DATE DUE

MAR 2 3 1983			
MAR 2 1983			
MAR - 3 1983			

DEMCO 38-297

FRAMES AND CAGES

FRAMES AND CAGES

The Repertory Grid Approach to
Human Understanding

By

ANTHONY RYLE

INTERNATIONAL UNIVERSITIES PRESS, INC

1975

Published by
International Universities Press, Inc.
239 Park Avenue South
New York, N.Y. 10003

ISBN 0 8236 2008 5

© Anthony Ryle 1975

Manufactured in Great Britain

Contents

I

Introduction

People are very hard to understand; all of us personally and some of us professionally devote a great deal of attention to the task of making sense of ourselves and others, but we are continually baffled by our failures to do so adequately. We respond to our failures in a number of ways; usually, and necessarily, by simplification and often by restricting our attention to only certain aspects—for example by separating thinking from feeling, by being concerned with either behaviour or with experience, by attending either to the individual or to the group, by looking either at form and process or at content—but in the end, in our personal lives at least, we are forced back, perhaps not always in full awareness, to considering all these aspects together. It is perhaps obvious that those setting out to teach, help or treat others cannot work with fragmented or partial views of man without failing or harming others, but the need to respond to the other with an adequately full and complex apprehension of his position is not exclusive to the professional, it is central to any human relationship.

Those we label neurotic or mentally ill have a particular difficulty in comprehending and communicating with others. Except when secondary to organic impairment, this difficulty is not a symptom—it is the fundamental problem—a problem often to be understood in terms of their personal histories, and differing in degree only from the universal human problem of relating. If we can accept that men have two important basic attributes—an innate and powerful drive to relate to others, and a continuing attempt to make sense of their experiences—then we can see that failures to satisfy the first drive may result from failure in the second area, that is to say from incomplete or distorted modes of making sense of the self and others. It is for this reason that the study of the concepts men hold of themselves and others, and the clarification of how they succeed or fail in communicating with each other, is of central psychological interest. This book describes the use of a psychological technique and considers some aspects of psychological theory which may have some contribution to make in this area. We will begin by considering the nature of the problem involved in communication.

The communication we achieve with others is based on the fact that the meanings of the words, gestures and symbolical actions we employ are, to an incomplete but adequate extent, shared. We are most sure of achieving communication when we are explicit about the language used, as for example, in formal logic or rigorous science, and we are most aware of communicating poorly when we lack a common language or where it is obvious that differences in experiences and culture are leading to differing interpretations of the language used. Between these extremes of clear, explicit communication and obviously imperfect communication, there lies a wide zone where more or less adequate understanding is achieved, but within which communication is impoverished or distorted to an extent, and in ways, that are not always apparent.

Unrecognised failure to communicate is most frequent in the exchanges of close personal relationships, for here our common language can conceal the degree to which our individual histories have left us with different assumptions and expectations. If the relationship between two people is likened to a voyage, then it is as if the two participants are using charts with the same titles, but with systematic differences of scale, shape and direction in respect of main features.

This book is about a recent development in psychology, the psychology of personal constructs (Kelly 1955) and about methods derived from this theory—the Repertory Grid (RG) technique—which allow the systematic exploration of the charts of others. It is mostly concerned with the use of the technique in the clinical setting, to understand and measure change in neurotic patients, but its application to the investigation of professional 'changers' (i.e. to psychotherapists and social workers) is also described. My own work has been carried out in the context of a University Health Service in which particular attention is paid to students' emotional and learning problems, and in which the therapeutic approach is based on a psychoanalytic, object-relations model, and this experience and bias have helped to determine the book's particular focus.

Psychoanalytically derived approaches to therapy have been increasingly concerned with the understanding of the patient's 'as if' system as it operates in the 'here and now', that is to say with identifying the characteristics of the patient's chart from his account of himself and his significant others, but above all from his on-going relationship with the therapist. One of the problems of evaluating psychoanalytic therapy is the essentially personal, subjective nature of the therapist's involvement with his patient; another is the difficult language-system of psychoanalysis, with its frequent references to higher order abstractions involving complex assumptions about personality development. One exciting potentiality of RG technique, in my opinion, is that it opens up some of the areas central to psychoanalytic understanding to a publicly accessible method of investigation. For this reason, the relationship of grid findings to clinical formulations based upon object-relations theory will be a recurrent theme. It would be a mistake to claim, however, that RG technique can be as revealing as the patient–therapist interaction, where much that is discovered depends upon the mutual exploration and teasing out of symbolism and the noting of indirect cues not initially accessible to language. Indeed, the putting of these aspects of the patient's experience into language may be an important part of the therapeutic task. The reliance upon language in the repertory grid technique, therefore, imposes inevitable limitations upon its scope.

How is it that we can use language to explore the particular meanings given to words by others when we are forced to rely upon shared language as our medium of enquiry? This conundrum is not a serious threat to repertory grid technique (or to conversation!) once one accepts that further exploration through the medium of language can refine the discriminations imposed. For example, a novice being taken sailing will understand quite clearly the meaning of 'rope' and there will be no failure in communication between him and the expert; in the course, however, of crewing the boat, he will have to learn to distinguish between 'sheets', 'halyards' and 'warps', and within 'sheets' between 'main' and 'jib' sheets, within 'halyards' between those for hoisting the 'mainsail' and the 'jib' and between 'warps' those appropriate for the 'bow' and the 'stern'. In this example, 'rope' was used in a consensual way, but the term was found to subsume a taxonomy of more detailed differentiated meanings. The word 'love' also has its consensual meaning, but the statement, 'I love Jemima

very deeply', could indicate many distinguishable affects and behaviours and further enquiry would be necessary before any real
understanding could be achieved. The RG technique involves the
subject in a formalised semantic exercise through which he defines
and differentiates between the range of possible meanings of the
terms he has used to make discriminations. To anticipate, the
technique consists essentially of systematically comparing elements
(in this case, people) against descriptions (constructs). From these
comparisons, the elements can be compared for overall similarity,
or for similarity on particular constructs, and the relationships
between the different constructs can be investigated. For example,
the meaning of 'love' in relation to Jemima might, after testing,
be elucidated as follows: 'I see from your test that you see Jemima
as, in many ways, very much like your mother.' (so far, element
relationships have been used to indicate the possible connotations
of loving.) 'I also notice that "love", for you, seems largely independent of sexual feeling and tends to be associated with a
feeling of suffocation.' (The people described in the RG test as
'loved' are not, in general, described as 'sexually attractive' and
are, in general, described as 'suffocating'.) We are now using the
subject's construct interrelations to explore the implications for
him of the meaning of 'to love'. Taken together, the grid evidence
might incline one to advise Jemima to watch out.

It is apparent that the language used by two individuals can
blur the meanings they intend to convey, but this blurring can be
explored and reduced by using language. In the formal language
of science, great emphasis is placed upon exactness, but in the
language of interpersonal transactions, we encounter a wider
range of possible subsumed meanings; perhaps we 'deliberately'
maintain a higher degree of ambiguity in this context. One task
of therapy may well be to help people achieve a less ambiguous
and more adequate and, hence, usually, a more complex taxonomy
of interpersonal language.

In the attempt to clarify the blurred edges of meaning, RG
technique relies on the use of words; but the test itself involves
numerical ratings and complex mathematical analysis. Numeracy
is not always highly developed in members of the caring profes-
sions, and the reduction of subtle shades of feeling to a sea of
figures, or to maps, may offend or confuse some readers. I hope
they will resist the temptation to close their eyes, or the book,
when figures or graphs start appearing, and make the attempt to

grasp the numerical and geographical versions or metaphors which RG technique generates—all of which will be explained in prose.

The title of the book deserves a word of explanation. Awareness of the ways in which our perceptions are differently moulded by our histories is now widespread. There is a prevalent fiction, derived from this awareness, that freedom can be achieved by rejecting all frameworks or by according equal virtue to any framework one cares to adopt. Such views are a part of the ideology of the 'alternative culture' and find expression in their most extreme form in the vagueness of the acid-head; they are seductive, but false. I would assert that there is no experience without structuring, and that greater freedom can only be achieved through increasing the complexity and subtlety of the frameworks of perception, in ways which expressly acknowledge the need to scan alternative constructions. The loosening, or loss of structuring achieved or experienced through the use of psychedelic drugs or in madness is not, in itself, liberating, though it may be true that some loosening of structure may be necessary before change and the elaboration of more complete structures can occur. Each framework through which we construe experience is capable of liberating us from a previous restriction of vision; but each, by excluding alternative structures, must also limit our possibilities and hence, to some degree, imprison us. There is no final solution to be found, either in the abolition of structures, or in the search for a perfect structure. The man who would enlarge his freedom must engage in a continuing attempt to increase the range and complexity of possible constructions open to him.

This book is addressed primarily to those professionally concerned with the assisting and measuring of change in patients and clients with personal difficulties; that is, to social workers, psychologists and psychiatrists. Most of the material presented is derived from work with patients diagnosed on clinical, and often on psychometric, criteria as neurotic. In most cases, the patients and also the controls who have been studied, were university students. However, the implications of RG technique and of the findings reported here extend beyond this narrow professional confine, and this technique is not dependent on having highly articulate subjects. By presenting in an accessible and explicit form evidence as to the ways in which each individual, in some degree, inhabits a unique corner of the world, RG studies can give illumination to all those with special needs or responsibilities for understanding others—for example, teachers and managers—and indeed to all of us struggling to make sense of personal relationships.

The book begins with a brief critical examination of Kelly's theory of personal constructs and the attempt to place this in relation to other theories used in the clinical setting. There follows a 'cook-book' account of RG test construction and a description of the sorts of measure yielded by the mathematical analysis of the grid. Following this, the psychological significance of these various measures is discussed and the evidence validating some of the inferences drawn from grid data is presented. The main body of the book is devoted to accounts of the use of grids to investigate a range of problems of psychological interest. Finally, some of the wider implications of RG findings are discussed.

Much of the research discussed in this book is my own, because the particular applications of RG techniques which have appealed to me have not attracted wide research interest except from Rowe (1969; 1971a, b, c). In the available general accounts of Kelly's work (Bannister & Mair 1968; Bannister & Fransella 1971) almost no attention is paid to element relationship—an omission which, in my view, greatly diminishes the potential of the techniques for helping our understanding of intrapsychic life and interpersonal relations.

In order to preserve confidentiality, case material is presented in ways which prevent identification of the subjects. The contribution of the unnamed two or three hundred who have completed grids for this research deserves acknowledgment. Most of the work was done while I was in receipt of personal grants from the Medical Research Council (M.R.C.) which have enabled me to have the assistance, first of Martin Lunghi, and latterly of Dana Breen. Both these colleagues have made major contributions of thought and effort to the development of the technique and the understanding of our findings. Finally, without the friendly advice and essential M.R.C. computer service of Dr Patrick Slater at the Institute of Psychiatry, the work could not have been done at all.

2

Kelly's Theory of Personal Constructs

Kelly worked as a teacher and counsellor and his theory grew out of his need, in the clinical and teaching setting, to understand, predict and have an effect upon his clients and students. One of his major contributions was to insist that this need to understand, predict and have an effect upon was not any monopoly of himself or of scientists in general, but was a fundamental attribute of the way in which men exist in the world. His theory rests upon the assumption that men are actively engaged in making sense of and extending their experience, an assumption which can account for the activities of the theorists. For Kelly, understanding another man is achieved to the extent that we know how he goes about the task of making sense of his world. The personal construct system which each man develops is the set of representations or models of the world he has developed, a set which is acquired through social experience, some of it pre-verbal, some of it verbally transmitted and not all of it accessible to the individual in terms of self-consciously held concepts. In all cases, this system is to some degree shared with others and to some degree unique to the individual. This personal construct system is not immutably fixed—as with the scientists' hypotheses, further experience may modify it.

The personal construct system is built up of interrelated constructs; each individual construct is concerned in discriminating between elements, an element being defined as anything which can be so compared or contrasted (for example, people, vegetables or concepts can all be elements). A construct can only be applied to elements which fall within the same class or, in Kelly's terms, range of convenience. Constructs, explicitly or implicitly, are always bi-polar; for example, URANIUM and PLUTONIUM are similar in being *radio-active* and different in this respect from LEAD which is *inert* or, to take another example, SEMANTICS and LINGUISTICS are similar in that they are both *concerned with language* and differ from STATISTICS which is about *mathematical associations*.* The constructs involved in these discriminations are *radioactive* versus *inert* and *mathematical* versus *to do with language*. Constructs are interrelated and organised in a structured system, and the relationships between constructs are relatively constant and systematic.

Kelly's theory is set out in terms of a fundamental postulate and a number of corollaries; these will now be given in full and subjected to critical comment:

FUNDAMENTAL POSTULATE

'A person's processes are psychologically channelled by the ways in which he anticipates events.'

CONSTRUCTION COROLLARY

'A person anticipates events by construing their replications.'

The content of this fundamental postulate and first corollary has been discussed above. Through them, Kelly expresses his assumption that all men act as scientists in the world. Leman (1970) has examined this aspect of Kelly's theory in the light of linguistic philosophy and suggests that Kelly's formulation of what constitutes science is somewhat overinfluenced by the hypothetico-deductive model. Leman proposes that 'the characteristically scientific activity is an operation with language . . . and that the scientist's most important problems have to do with the relationship between language and extra-linguistic reality . . .' This essay of Leman's, which represents a valuable critical account of Kelly's work, is summed up in the same paper as follows:

> What I have tried to suggest here, is that we (collectively and individually) live, not so much in the world, as in a model of the world made of words and word-like things . . . Collectively as 'Man', we have to try to correct and complete this linguistic model of extra-linguistic reality into a comprehensive and reliable operating manual for space-ship Earth, which we did not build, whirling through a cosmos we did not design; individually, as you or me, we have to try to complete and correct our individual linguistic models of our own

* Throughout the book we will observe the convention of writing ELEMENTS in capitals and *constructs* in italics.

extralinguistic realities into a comprehensive and reliable operating manual for flesh-ship Me, which we did not mould, 'thrown' (as the Existentialists say) into a world we did not make.

This formulation gets away from Kelly's preoccupation with prediction and control and emphasises more the making-sense-of aspect of men's construing of themselves and of reality.

INDIVIDUALITY COROLLARY

'Persons differ from each other in their construction of events.'

This corollary expresses the fact that each individual, in his unique experience, develops a unique model. As such, the corollary is a corrective to the naive assumption that outer reality is more or less directly, and similarly, represented by each person's grasp of it; or the equally naive and, to a degree, universal tendency to over-generalise from one's own experience to that of others. In my view, however, this corollary would be strengthened by the additional paradoxical statement that 'persons *resemble* each other in their construction of events'. Kelly paid rather little attention to developmental and social processes, and, while acknowledging the role of learning and culture in the acquisition of modes of construing the world, his own concern was largely with identifying the personal and not the social. A greater emphasis upon the degree to which construction systems are common would link with Leman's comments, noted above: the power of socially acquired language to set patterns and limits upon personal construing can hardly be overestimated, and indeed, without it, communication through speech would be impossible. Nonetheless, Kelly's insistence on the individual person was a healthy corrective to the strong tendency in much of psychology to avoid studying individual differences.

ORGANISATION COROLLARY

'Each person characteristically evolves, for his convenience in anticipating events, a construction system embracing ordinal relationships between constructs.'

In this part of his theory, Kelly is describing the way in which constructs are systematically interrelated and the way in which the system is organised. However, his formulations in this area include some ambiguities which have led to confusion. This confusion rests upon the fact that, in his discussion of the ordinal relationships of superordinate and subordinate constructs, two quite separate forms of relationship are described. One form of superordinacy is what I call the 'more general'; certain constructs, while still serving to differentiate between the same elements, do so at a higher level of generality. The second form of superordinacy is concerned with the construing of constructs; in this case, the construct becomes a special form of element. Here, the superordinate construct construes constructs but *cannot itself be employed* to construe the elements which are in the field of convenience of these subordinate constructs. This distinction is discussed more fully in Chapter 13.

DICHOTOMY COROLLARY

'A person's construction system is composed of a finite number of dichotomous constructs.'

This statement emphasises that every description or prediction has, explicitly or implicitly, a contrast pole. Where this is not stated explicitly, it may be important to identify it correctly if misconceptions are to be avoided. Individuals are not always aware of the implicit poles of constructs which they employ.

CHOICE COROLLARY

'A person chooses for himself that alternative in a dichotomised construct through which he anticipates a greater possibility for extension and definition of his system.'

This corollary embodies Kelly's assumption of man as being actively engaged in acting on the world rather than as simply reacting to it, and embodies a philosophical position which Kelly calls 'constructive alternatism'. It does not imply, of course, that men always construe the possibilities for extension correctly, i.e. in ways leading to real extension. As a theoretical assumption, this corollary represents a rejection of stimulus-response and reinforcement by drive-reduction models of human behaviour; and, as such, it is perhaps to be seen as a liberating overstatement rather than as an adequate account of all human behaviour, although it may be that it identifies correctly those aspects of behaviour which are characteristically human as opposed to animal.

Range Corollary

'A construct is convenient for the anticipation of a finite range of events only.'

This is a necessary part of the formal theory. A given construct can only be used appropriately to construe a limited range or class of elements. It is important, incidentally, to recognise that the words used to express the distinctions implied by constructs may be employed in quite distinct fields of convenience; words label the poles of constructs, but are not themselves the constructs.

Experience Corollary

'A person's construction system varies as he successively construes the replication of events.'

Here Kelly is again describing the 'scientific' operation of hypothesis testing, whereby the model is revised or confirmed, depending upon whether predictions are confirmed or fulfilled. While this aspect of the theory, allowing for a change in learning at a subtle and complex level, provides a more adequate model for the effects of much human experience, it needs to be recognised also that humans exhibit a capacity *not* to learn from experience. This resistance to change, described, in psychodynamic terms, as representing the operation of defences or of the compulsion to repeat, could be seen in personal construct terms as representing a relative inertia of the construct system.

Modulation Corollary

'The variation in a person's construction system is limited by the permeability of the constructs within whose ranges of convenience the variants lie.'

This represents an attempt to explain this relative resistance to change. This corollary, however, seems to be a largely tautological statement.

Fragmentation Corollary

'A person may successively employ a variety of construction sub-systems which are inferentially incompatible with each other.'

This aspect of Kelly's theory is needed to account for the observable fact that people can hold beliefs or make judgments which are not logically or inferentially compatible with each other. This incompatibility may be contained by the subject through the use of an appropriate superordinate construct; for example, a father's 'it hurts me more than it hurts you' may represent self-justification, his need to see himself as loving while he is beating his child being met by reference to a superordinate construct to do with moral duty. How adequately this formulation of Kelly's can deal with the phenomena of ambivalence, repression, dissociation and with the various other distortions of judgment and perception identifiable in neurotics and described in psychodynamic terms under the rubric of the various defence mechanisms is, I think, doubtful. Certainly, for myself, object-relations theory provides a more adequate model for construing these phenomena, although it is evident that many of the formulations of object-relations theory can be translated into personal construct terms. The recognition of features in the results of repertory grid testing which give evidence of these processes will be discussed later in the book.

COMMONALITY COROLLARY

'To the extent that one person employs a construction of experience which is similar to that employed by another, his psychological processes are similar to those of the other person.'

SOCIALITY COROLLARY

'To the extent that one person construes the construction processes of another, he may play a role in a social process involving the other person.'

In these two corollaries, Kelly emphasises what, in his terms, are the essential features of psychological similarity and of communication, and in the sociality corollary he provides what is probably the best available criterion for the measurement of empathy. These corollaries emphasise that it is in the sharing and understanding of the sytem used for comparing and contrasting phenomena that similarity and understanding are rooted. The part played by language and culture in contributing to similarity and understanding is little explored by Kelly. His concept of role, it will be observed, does not involve simply assuming a part or function in relation to the other; it also involves actively attempting to construe the other's way of construing.

From the above summary of Kelly's theory, it will be apparent that he aimed to set up a well-integrated set of propositions capable of testing and able to subsume or replace other psychological models. The best full account of this theory is provided by Kelly himself in his original work (Kelly 1955) of which the main argument is set out in a separately published paperback (Kelly 1963). Later accounts of the theory and reviews of much of the literature describing work in the tradition have been published in books by Bannister & Mair (1968) and Bannister & Fransella (1971); the review by Slater of the former book (Slater 1969) provides a balance to these accounts and draws attention to some omissions and some excessive claims made by these writers. Despite the enthusiasm of many followers of Kelly and despite the fact that a fairly large body of useful work has been carried out using repertory grid methods derived from personal construct theory, the theory itself has not attracted a great deal of attention, and empirical validation of the various propositions have been few. How far this is due to the inertia of 'man as scientist', faced with new ideas and how far to some irrelevancies or inadequacies in aspects of the theory it is difficult to determine. As regards its adequacy, it is clear that there are many shortcomings, as has already been indicated. For a more detailed critique, papers by Holland (1970), Leman (1970) and Shotter (1970) should be consulted. In order to consider the relevance of the theory for clinical work, it is necessary to consider it in relation to the other theories used in the clinical field and also to consider its relation to psychology as a whole. This is to be the subject matter of the next chapter.

3

The Relationship of
Personal Construct Theory to
Other Theories

However wide the implications of Kelly's theory, it was generated in the clinic and it is with its clinical applications that this book is largely concerned. It is therefore important to locate Kelly's position with reference to the other theories or models which form the basis of clinical practice.

In Britain, three main approaches may be identified: the medical, the behaviourist or learning theory model and the psychoanalytic model. Rogers's client-centred therapy, a fourth contender, has very little influence in this country. At the risk of considerable over-simplification, the relative positions of these approaches and of Kelly's along the following dimensions will be considered: (1) How far is the approach concerned with innate biological factors as opposed to acquired social factors; (2) How far is the approach concerned to account for the present state of an individual in terms of his past history and development; (3) How far does the approach describe man as reactive, responding to the world, and how far as exploring and acting on the world; (4) How far is the account of man given from the outside, describing behaviour rather than from the inside, describing experience; (5) How much importance is accorded to language, symbolism and the unconscious; (6) What are the implications of the theory for treatment.

INNATE BIOLOGICAL VERSUS ACQUIRED AND SOCIAL

Of the four models, the medical one is the one most focused upon innate and biological factors. Much early psychiatry was concerned with organically based psychological disorder and much effort is still devoted to identifying physical accompaniments or causes of mental disease, nowadays through genetic and biochemical investigation. The learning theory model also has a biological focus in so far as its approach is to man as an organism and it tends to be identified with simple dimensional models of personality, presumed to be innate. However, in so far as it is centrally concerned with learning, it can hardly avoid some acknowledgment of social processes. In clinical practice, however, its most successful application is in the treatment of phobias of situations or objects rather than in the modification of the social relationships of the patient—though the two may be connected. Psychoanalytic theory, while recognising genetically determined innate differences between individuals, and despite an early attempt to identify with the medical–biological model, is essentially concerned with the social processes, notably the effects of the earliest relationships upon later ones. In treatment, the modification of these effects through the social relationship between the patient and therapist is central. Kelly is concerned with the current situation and how the patient construes himself within it, and hence is solely concerned with social process, although he is not much concerned with how the patient's particular system was acquired.

STATIC VERSUS DEVELOPMENTAL

The medical model tends to regard an illness as an episode afflicting an organism which may or may not be predisposed, either by virtue of noxious experience or genetic predisposition. Learning theory, while explaining symptoms in terms of learnt experience, has no formally elaborated general theory of development. However, much work has been carried out in the learning theory tradition which is of relevance to development; for example, the study of the role of anxiety reduction as a secondary re-inforcer (e.g. Mowrer 1950) and studies of sex-role identification (e.g. Kagan (1958). Much of this work shows convergences with dynamic psychiatric theories, despite the very different languages Psychoanalysis is so centrally concerned with development tha its language tends to unite descriptive and developmental explanations in single terms, a habit which makes much psychoanalytic writing impenetrable and annoying to those not agreeing with the underlying assumptions. It was, however, in this attempt to construct a model to explain the experiences of adults by reference to childhood that psychoanalysis made its greatest contribution. To reconstruct experience we have to rely upon the accounts people give of it and not upon observations from outside. These accounts are, inevitably, most garbled and most distorted when they refer to the earliest experiences of the pre-verbal infant. In trying to reconstruct this experience, the analyst, like the cosmologist, is presented with a universe at one point in time and must attempt, from what he sees there, to explain how it came to reach its present state and to predict what its future development might be. That cosmology is a respectable science and psychoanalysis is not is partly, no doubt, due to the resistances which analysts postulate, but may also be due to the obscurity and variety of models generated during the history of psychoanalysis. However, this obscurity and variety, reminiscent, perhaps, of medieval cosmology, has also generated a large number of creative ideas. Kelly did not concern himself with the origin of man's world view and was dismissive of that version of analysis with which he showed any familiarity. He was interested in men as cosmologists of their own universe, but not much concerned with the history of their individual cosmological theories.

Man as Reactive versus Man as Agent

The main medical tradition would tend to emphasise the patient as someone to whom an illness has happened; to speak, for example, of a case of depression, not a depressed man; and the treatments used will also tend to emphasise the passivity of the patient as a recipient of drugs or electric shocks or whatever. The same approach marks most learning theory practitioners. Behaviour modification implies the therapist doing something to the patient rather than with the patient, a distinction of little importance in the case of treatment of irritating habits, but more contentious in the case of social behaviours. Psychoanalysis can also, through the induced dependency of the patient and the controlling passivity of the analyst, diminish the patient's sense of his own capacity to act, but this would not be characteristic of most psychoanalytic therapies. The aim of psychoanalytically based therapy or of analysis is to free the patient's self from inner constraints and to increase his power for independent action. Of the four approaches, Kelly's is the most explicit and most emphatic in insisting that the only adequate model of a man is of somebody acting upon the world and actively attempting to confirm and extend his construction of it.

OUTSIDE VERSUS INSIDE VIEWS OF MAN

The medical model, even when not based upon the assumption that physical causes must underlie mental disorder, tends to pay most attention to observable departures from the norm, but because so much of the symptomatology of psychiatric illness is in the patient's experience, psychiatrists inevitably attend in some way to what it feels like to be the patient. Crude learning theory would reduce man to a point on the line between a stimulus and a response. In its most complex modifications, one finds increasingly adequate elaborations of the model of the organism interposed between the stimulus and the response, but a learning theorist would still hesitate before attributing intention to this organism and would not take seriously a question about the organism's relationship with itself. Psychoanalysis and Kelly have in common a concentration upon the individual's own unique apprehension of the world and with how this apprehension can, if distorted, be the kernel of his sickness.

LANGUAGE SYMBOLS AND THE UNCONSCIOUS

The unconscious is a concept invented, or at least, made important by psychoanalysis and largely ignored or rejected by the medical and learning theory models of illness. Metaphors and models used to describe the unconscious have varied and evolved in the history of psychoanalytic thought, but the common intent of all the varied formulations has been to help the analyst and patient reconstruct and put into words those aspects of the individual's past experience which continue to modify his perception and behaviours. The identification and naming of the unspoken inaccessible 'as if' system which dominates some aspects of behaviour is a central task of analytic therapy. Lacan (1966), the French analyst, describes the unconscious in the following terms:*

> The unconscious is that chapter of my history which is denoted by a blank, or filled with a lie. It is the censored chapter, but the truth can be rediscovered. In most cases, it is written elsewhere; by 'elsewhere' I mean: (1) In surviving monuments: in this instance, my body; that is to say, the hysterical nucleus of neurosis in which the symptom displays the structure of a language and can be deciphered in the

* I am grateful to George Craig for this translation.

manner of an inscription which, once it has been recorded, may without serious loss, be destroyed; (2) In archival documents: in this case my childhood memories, quite as impenetrable as any documents when I am unaware of their source; (3) In evolving semantic patterns; this corresponds to the stock list of and to the individual sense given to the words which make up the vocabulary which is specific to me, as it does to my life-style and to my character; (4) In traditions, too, even legends which, recast in a heroic mould, are the vehicle of my history; (5) In the direct traces of that history which are inevitably preserved despite the subsequent distortions occasioned by the need to accommodate the adulterated chapter with the chapters flanking it. The meaning of these traces is what my exegesis will re-establish.

Kelly rejected the concept of the unconscious but provided in his own terms a number of equivalent formulations for those processes attributed to unconscious factors. Thus, his recognition that constructs may operate in pre-verbal, non-symbolised ways, could be taken to describe much which an analyst would describe as representing unconscious factors. Inadequate or inappropriate superordinate constructs of the construct-construing type, highly impermeable constructs and constructs of which the implicit pole is 'submerged' all represent personal construct formulations which can be seen to be equivalent to some aspects of unconscious process. The question of personal construct equivalencies of unconscious processes is further discussed later in the book. Meanwhile, it should be noted that both Kelly and the psychoanalyst (with his emphasis in therapy upon the here and now interaction of patient and therapist) share a concern to identify and put into words those constructs which are being used by the patient, and to enlarge and make more adequately complex the patient's construct system.

IMPLICATIONS FOR THERAPY

Therapy within the medical model would be directed to the cause of the disorder, where this is known, or to the use of remedies known empirically to cure or relieve the symptoms of the disorder. Treatment will have a physiological focus, and the doctor's psychological role is one of giving support and, perhaps, explanation as in the care and treatment of physical disorder. In practice based on learning theory, the patient would be given an explanation of the treatment and will then agree to expose himself to the de-conditionting, aversive or behaviour-modifying procedures. The doctor's authority in prescribing treatment is accepted much as in the medical model. In psychoanalysis, the therapist will attempt to avoid accepting any of the roles with which the patient may invest him. He will embark on a relationship with the patient, the understanding and evolution of which is the central process of therapy. How he embarks on this process, and the degree of self-exposure which he himself allows will differ greatly between different therapists. Learning takes place in this process through the corrective emotional experience of the interpreted transference relationship. It is through this process that unconscious primitive fantasies are replaced by freer and less idiosyncratic apprehension of the self and the world.

The implications of personal construct theory for therapy, in Kelly's view, were to suggest various forms of treatment in which the patient or client was encouraged to deliberately play various roles (see Bonarius 1970). However, very little has been written up of the practicability or efficacy of this treatment approach. A good deal that goes on in Rogerian counselling and in brief psychotherapy can be usefully examined and easily described in personal construct terms, but the theory cannot be said to have generated an active therapeutic programme at present.

The Comparison of the Different Models

The above discussion of personal construct theory in relation to other models has been, of necessity, brutally short; but may serve to place personal construct theory in context for those who are unfamiliar with it. In summary, one could say that Kelly is distant from the medical model, formally opposed to the learning theory model and shows considerable overlap with the psychoanalytic model, however much he may have rejected psychoanalysis as a theoretical system and however far his propositions are stated in a totally different language. Kelly, however, does not share with psychoanalysis a preoccupation with the effects of early experience and has not himself provided any developmental theory, although an approach combining Piaget's and Kelly's thoughts might well be fruitful. Nor does Kelly effectively provide an alternative therapeutic method.

These different models compete to some degree, but may also

be seen to have, in Kelly's terms, different ranges of convenience. Certainly, the medical model can be contrasted with the psychoanalytic model in that the former is decreasingly, and the latter increasingly relevant as one moves from organic brain syndromes through the functional psychoses into the neurotic and personality disorders. On this spectrum, too, Kelly's relevance is at the same end as is that of psychoanalysis, and may be as readily extended to the understanding of the normal.

Kelly and Psychological Tradition

Having attempted to place Kelly in the context of competing or complementary psychological theories which are applied to the understanding of man in the clinical context, a brief reference to his place in the psychological tradition may be appropriate. His followers make much of his departure from many of the positions held by orthodox psychologists and, doubtless, many orthodox psychologists themselves see this departure as a matter for regret rather than for praise. Kelly himself was in reaction against that part of the psychological tradition which reduced man as subject to a level below man as psychologist, and which, as he argued, left man as psychologist unexplained. The problem of the reflexive nature of psychological theory was not, of course, a new one; but useful consideration of the problems involved may have been made difficult by the split in psychology in which the more academic approach appeared to diminish man, whereas the psychoanalytical approach appeared to ignore science. In fact, much of what Kelly wrote may be found expressed with equal clarity and vigour in the writing of William James, a predecessor of such weight that it is surprising to find that he is virtually unmentioned by Kelly and his main protagonists (Bannister & Mair 1968). For example, in his last book, *Some Problems of Philosophy* (1911), James insists upon the essential similarity of philosophical, scientific and ordinary thinking in the following passage. (p. 15):

> Philosophy in the full sense is only man thinking, thinking about generalities rather than about particulars. Whether about generalities or particulars, man thinks always by the same methods. He observes, discriminates, generalises, classifies, looks for causes, traces analogies and makes hypotheses. Philosophy, taken as something distinct from science,

or from practical affairs, follows no method peculiar to itself. All our thinking today has evolved gradually out of primitive human thought, and the only really important changes that have come over its manner (as distinguished from the matters in which it believes) are a greater hesitancy in asserting its convictions and a habit of seeking verification for them whenever it can.

Later (p. 67), in discussing what he calls 'our conceptual translation of the perceptual flux', James foreshadows Kelly's description of the construct system:

> . . . the concepts in the explanatory system must . . . harmoniously 'connect'. What does this mean? . . . It points to the fact that, when concepts of various sorts are once abstracted or constructed, new relations are then found between them, connecting them in peculiarly intimate 'rational' and unchangeable ways. In another book, I have tried to show that these irrational relations are all products of our faculty of comparison and of our sense of 'more'.

Later, he writes: '. . . in general, one may say that the perception of likeness and unlikeness generates the whole of "rational" or "necessary" truth.' Towards the end of the book, in his chapter on novelty and causation, James betrays the same irritation as Kelly with theories which deny man's capacity to invent and create.

It seems, therefore, that Kelly, rather than representing an entirely new departure in psychology, can be seen to be rediscovering, in his emphasis and concentration on that which is specifically human, an aspect of psychology lost in the pseudo-scientific objectification of man which crude behaviourism represented. In this rediscovery, Kelly often adopts positions which are themselves naive, overstated and overpolemical. His neglect of the social basis of language and of learning, his lack of attention to developmental processes and his dismissal or incomprehension of phenomenology and of psychoanalysis (discussed by Holland 1970) are all evidence of limitations which cannot be ignored. The form of theory he began to build may be extended and developed to provide a more adequate account, even perhaps, as enthusiasts claim, an account which can subsume other psychological theories, but I believe that Bannister and Mair are premature in their attempt to instal personal construct theory, in its present form, as a fully satisfying and internally consistent system.

For all its defects, however, the orientation which Kelly adopted shows many similarities with other intellectual movements of the present century, even though there is little evidence of direct derivation or interaction. These approaches have in common an emphasis upon the activity of man in perceiving, structuring and making sense of his environment and experience, and a central concern for those processes, individual and social, which determine how this creative apperception is carried out. Kelly can claim kinship with workers in many fields—for example with Lévi Strauss (1966) in anthropology, with those concerned with the sociology of knowledge (for example Berger & Luckman 1967), with the modern linguistic work associated with Chomsky (1968), with contemporary developments in artificial intelligence (Clowes 1972) and with the contribution made to art history and criticism by Gombrich (1960).

It is not my intention, and not within my competence, to pursue these connections in this book, however. Here, my main concern will be with the narrower clinical field and, to some extent, with teaching, and in terms of theoretical systems the main focus will be upon the connections between personal construct theory and psychoanalysis, for it seems possible that, in the future, developments in personal construct theory may play an important role in meeting the challenge to build a bridge between social psychology and psychoanalysis, the need for which Jahoda (1972) outlines and summarises in the following passage:

> Psychoanalysis challenges social psychology above all to strive after statements with content rather than formalism; to recognise that it has neglected systematic description of social life and to compensate for this; to be less concerned with academic respectability and more with meaningful problems; to examine its conception of man, who is neither altogether driven, nor altogether master of his fate; and to transgress deliberately into adjacent fields not with the intention of usurping them, but in order to test the power of its own contribution.

If personal construct theory is to fulfil this bridging role, I believe it has to come to terms much more fully than is now the case with the ways in which man is 'not altogether master of his fate' and this means taking account of contributions from both behaviourism and psychoanalysis. The challenge of psychoanalysis is, I believe, the larger one; psychoanalysis alone has an adequate approach to the task of understanding man's personal history and personal creativity.

I believe the meeting point of personal construct theory and of psychoanalytic theory is a fruitful one. This book, of course, is not concerned with the ultimate clash or marriage between the theories, so much as with attempts at cross-fertilization at the level of detailed studies of individual cases. The greater part of the book is devoted to studies using the repertory grid technique which Kelly initiated, but interpreting the findings of experiments using this technique in the light of both personal construct, and of object-relations psychoanalytic theory. That this approach may please neither avowed Kellyans nor dedicated psychoanalysts is, of course, more than likely.

4

Repertory Grid Construction:
The Basic Technique

It will be easier to explain the nature of a repertory grid if a simplified example is provided. Let us suppose that a young lady, who might be the heroine of a Victorian novelette, is considering the personal qualities of the eligible men in her social circle. If we were to ask her tactfully, she might be prepared to name the gentlemen and, if we then invited her to compare and contrast them, we would be able to identify, from her choice of terms, which personal qualities seemed of most importance to her in the evaluation of men. Let us assume that the men in question are the curate, the local squire, a young army officer, and the owner of a nearby coal-mine, and that the attributes she selects as most important in distinguishing between these men are youthfulness, being admirable, being religious, being wealthy, and being approved of by mama. It is safe to assume that even the least mathematical of heroines would be able to compare each of these men with the others on each of these qualities. To construct a repertory grid test from these data, these comparisons must be expressed in some mathematical form. This can be achieved by dividing the four men into the two most and two least well-described by each quality, or by ranking them on each quality, or by rating or scoring each man on each quality on some agreed scale. For the purpose of argument let us choose the latter method, using a five-point scale—the higher score implying that the individual is well-described by the given description. One possible set of judgments for our heroine is summarised in Table 4.1.

These rows and columns of figures are an example of a repertory grid. What does it tell us about our heroine? By noting the men selected and the qualities about which judgments are made, and by a simple inspection of the grid, we can learn something about the heroine's social position and something about her views of the curate, squire, army officer and coal-owner. Indirectly, and

Table 4.1

Constructs	CURATE	SQUIRE	OFFICER	COAL-OWNER
Youthful	4	2	5	2
Admired	3	2	5	1
Religious	5	4	3	3
Wealthy	2	4	1	5
Approved of by mama	2	4	1	4

of greater interest, we can deduce a good deal more about the heroine herself. In particular, if we compare the scores in the different rows of this table, we learn something about the inter-connections which exist for her between the different qualities she has used to describe the men. We can observe, for example, that those rated one way for *admired* tend to be rated the opposite way for *wealthy, religious* and (alas!) for *approved of by mama*. From these connections, we can begin to understand the heroine and predict the possible developments of the plot.

In reality, it would be dangerous to deduce too much from so small a grid, and the interpretation of the figures in a large grid demands more than simple inspection. But this example serves to illustrate the essential components and conventions of the grid, namely that it is made up of a list of things to be compared: the elements; and a list of terms used to compare and contrast them —called the constructs; the first list being compared systematically against the second list to generate the grid of figures which gives this technique its name. Because of the essentially bi-polar nature of constructs, Kelly and many others since consider that constructs should be elicited in a bi-polar form. To achieve this, our subject, when she described an element as, say, *religious*, would be asked to name the contrasting quality which might, for example, be *agnostic* for one subject or *adventurous* for another. The elements would then be rated on the construct *religious versus agnostic* or *religious versus adventurous*.

As the essential feature of the RG technique is that the subject compares a list of elements on a list of constructs, the elements must be comparable. One cannot, for example, compare people, vegetables and concepts with each other using the same terms. By the same token, the constructs must be equally applicable to all the elements.

TEST CONSTRUCTION

The first task of the person carrying out RG testing is to elicit from, or provide for, the subject doing the test a list of comparable elements and of relevant and usable constructs. How these lists are achieved will depend to some degree upon the questions which are to be answered by the investigator, but in general, the more the subject provides his own elements and constructs, the more he reveals to the tester about himself. The tester, however, is bound to exert some influence at this stage. For example, should he plan to investigate how the subject would go about choosing a football team, he would probably wish to limit the element list to footballers; while if he were concerned to explain the subject's masochistic behaviour, he would wish to have as elements all those emotionally significant other people known to the subject. In a clinical situation, of course, the latter model is the usual one, and in most tests discussed in this book the element lists are made up of significant other people named by the subject. For some purposes, the tester may ask the subject to include specific figures; for example, 'your mother', 'your spouse', 'your doctor'; or he may indicate by description or role-title, certain sorts of person; for example, 'someone of your own age whom you dislike', or 'the teacher you most admire'. This ensures a reasonable spread of elements, including, for example, elements of both sexes, different generations and both liked and disliked people, but it should be noted that to structure the test in this way may already lead to some loss of information, for the subject who only provides elements of one sex or one generation, or who includes no disliked figures, is already telling you something about himself. Another type of element which may be included at the tester's request is the ideal figure; the inclusion of elements such as 'the sort of person you would like to be' or 'the kind of person who could help you' may be of value in exploring some questions.

Elements may, therefore, be elicited from the subject or provided by the tester; or both methods may be used in combination. Whichever way is adopted, the first stage in construing a test is to assemble a list of elements. The next step is to elicit the constructs, and here the value of leaving as much as possible to the subject is even greater. In the classical method described by Kelly, constructs are elicited by the tester choosing, at random, sets of three elements from the subject's element list and asking the subject to describe all the ways in which one of the elements in this triad resembles another and differs from the third. As this process is carried out, the tester notes down all the descriptions of similarity and difference used by the subject. Successive triads of elements are used until no new constructs are being elicited. The use of three rather than two elements in this procedure is based upon Kelly's insistence on the bi-polar nature of constructs, and the fact that three elements are the minimum necessary to permit recognition of both similarities and differences and to elicit the terms defining both poles of the construct. Thus, the construct *white versus black* is different from *white versus coloured*, and failure to elicit the contrast pole of the construct *white* as used by the subject, could mislead the tester. In practice, constructs can be quite satisfactorily elicited using only pairs of elements, the tester asking the subject to name both similarities and differences; and in completing the grid, subjects can be asked to rate elements against unipolar constructs according to how far they apply to the elements, for, in the final analysis of the grid, the implicit pole of all constructs will be apparent from the way in which the subject has used them and can be identified from the construct correlations. This slightly simple procedure seems reasonable as subjects are unlikely, in rating a set of elements against a unipolar construct, to vary the implicit pole of the construct employed.

During the eliciting of constructs, the tester must decide whether or not to play any part in prompting as to which type of construct might usefully be included. For example, in comparing significant other people, one subject might produce only descriptive, emotionally neutral constructs such as *middle-aged, works with his hands, tall*. This is clearly news about the subject, but one might feel that it was due to uncertainty or misunderstanding about the tester's intentions, in which case, prompts like 'Can you tell me how your feelings for A and B differ?' may lead to the production of constructs with greater affective content. With most subjects, the procedure of comparing five or six triads of elements to elicit constructs leads to the production of fifteen to thirty constructs, after which repetitions or simple paraphrases begin to appear. These constructs are recorded in the subject's own words In practice, the use of supplied constructs to describe common judgments enables comparisons between individuals to be more easily carried out. Whenever constructs are supplied, however, it is best to allow the subject to modify these constructs if, in their supplied form, he does not feel able to use them. It is silly to try to understand someone's way of making sense of the world by making him use constructs which do not make sense to him. In general, subjects' use of supplied and elicited constructs does not differ crucially, though the latter may be used more differentially (Adams-Webber 1970).

At this point, the tester has assembled a list of elements and a list of constructs elicited from the subject. The completion of the test requires no more than that the subject be asked to compare, or rate, all the people on all the constructs, either by dichotomising (this is rarely used as it is relatively insensitive), by ranking, or by rating. My own preference is for rating, scores of 1–5 or 1–7 being given by the subject to each element on each construct, according to how far the element is correctly described by the construct. The form in which the test is assembled can be a simple affair of rows and columns, as in the completed heroine's example given earlier in this chapter. Alternatively, the elements can be listed and numbered, and a small booklet can be made up with one page for each construct. The subject writes element numbers on this page, either in the appropriate columns if a rating method is being used, or in the appropriate order if a ranking method is being used. The virtue of this form is that it ensures that subjects work by comparing elements on each construct in turn rather than by rating the elements in turn on all the constructs. This is preferable as it means that the elements are, in effect, being compared rather than rated against descriptions.*

In the form of grid described so far, which I will call from now onwards the 'standard grid', the elements are people known to the subject. In completing a test of this sort, the subject has to make an overall judgment about each person on each construct, and this can be difficult. For example, in rating William on the construct *affectionate*, it is not possible to take account of the fact that William is relatively very affectionate to Mary, but somewhat cool towards Anne. In order to allow the subject to make this kind of distinction, some modifications to the standard technique have been developed. One method is to allow for multiple ratings of a given element, usually the SELF; thus, the SELF might be rated under a number of conditions, such as YOURSELF WHEN

---

* Subjects completing the same grid by rating each element in turn on all the constructs, rather than setting the elements against each construct in turn, generate markedly different grids according to J. Tutton (personal communication).

HAPPY, YOURSELF WHEN SAD, YOURSELF AT HOME, YOURSELF AT WORK, YOURSELF LAST YEAR, YOURSELF NOW, YOURSELF AS YOU REALLY ARE, YOURSELF AS YOU WOULD LIKE TO BE, YOURSELF WITH MARY, or YOURSELF WITH ANNE. A further version of this method asks the subject to rate himself as he believes others see him; for example, YOURSELF AS WILLIAM SEES YOU, YOURSELF AS MARY SEES YOU, YOURSELF AS ANNE SEES YOU, and so on. These two variants can be called the multiple-self and the multiple-self-as-perceived variations of the standard grid. A second variation in technique, with larger implications, is the Dyad Grid (Ryle & Lunghi 1970). In this form of test, the elements are not people; instead they are the relationships between pairs. Thus, if we had wished to give our heroine a grid of this sort, the elements would have been YOURSELF IN RELATION TO THE CURATE, THE CURATE IN RELATION TO YOU, YOURSELF IN RELATION TO THE SQUIRE, THE SQUIRE IN RELATION TO YOU, and so on. In eliciting constructs for the dyad form of the test, the use of triads of relationship elements is too complicated, and pairs of elements are preferable. The form of elicitation would be as follows: 'Can you tell me ways in which your relationship to the squire resembles or differs from the curate's relationship to you?' and so on. Constructs must be phrased to describe interaction, thus with the dyad grid, the construct *admirable* could take the forms *admires* or *is admired by*. Each pair of persons included in the grid would generate two elements, i.e. SELF-to-SQUIRE and SQUIRE-to-SELF. In most cases, a number of dyads in which the subject figures will be included because this can provide evidence of how he sees his own role to be differentiated in different relationships. The inclusion of various other pairs can provide evidence of what models of dyadic relationships are available to him. However, to explore the full potential of either the standard or the dyad grid requires, in the first instance, a discussion of the ways in which grid data are processed to produce measures of psychological interest, and this is the subject matter of the next chapter.

5

The Mathematical Analysis
of the Repertory Grid

The point of psychological testing in general and of grids in particular, is to enable the subject to communicate matters relevant to those aspects of his psychology which are under investigation and to abstract from all his communication measures of the most significant aspects. As already described, a grid may be derived from splitting (dichotomising), ranking, or rating elements on constructs. Splitting is a relatively crude method, but simpler to analyse; ranking or rating present the experimenter with rows and columns of figures in which each number represents the subject's judgment applied to an element, that is to say it represents an interaction between a construct and an element. In this form, the data are too complex to be accessible to inspection, and some form of analysis and display is required before conclusions can be drawn or interpretations made. Even if simple dichotomisation of the elements on each construct is being used rather than ranking or rating, some form of mathematical analysis is required.

The object of the mathematical analysis of a grid must be to reveal the structure in the grid, not to impose the experimenter's structure upon it. If each figure on the grid represented an independent, unconnected judgment of the subject, there would be no structure to reveal; but in fact, all grids produced by men are characterised by structure, that is to say, there are relationships between individual ratings which are accessible to mathematical analysis, and which are related to underlying psychological processes.

Full analysis of the essential properties of a grid in terms of the relationships between constructs, the relationships between elements and the interaction of elements and constructs demands computer analysis. Simpler methods of analysis are described in Bannister & Mair (1968) and are fairly easily applied to grids based on dichotomisation of elements. There seems little advantage in using these methods where more comprehensive use can be made of the data by a fuller analysis. In particular, element relationships and construct–element interaction are only fully explored by the full analysis, and problems of centrality versus extremity of ratings and of skew distribution of elements on constructs cannot easily be dealt with except through the computer analysis. For a number of years, research workers have had access to the computer services of the M.R.C. Unit for the processing of repertory grids under Patrick Slater, where successive 'Ingrid' programs have been developed. The latest of these (Ingrid 72) is now available, restricted to a maximum of 25 elements and 25 constructs, for the use of psychologists and psychiatrists. Full details of the procedures involved in the Ingrid analysis are available in a number of publications obtainable from The Institute of Psychiatry and listed at the end of this chapter. A very brief account is given in Slater (1969). The requirements are defined as follows:

> Grids accepted for analysis in the service provided by the Medical Research Council may refer to any set of elements selected to cover the range of convenience which is of interest in the case. Any procedure can be used to obtain the constructs. Evaluation may be expressed on any numerical scale. Some such procedures and scales may be less sensitive than others to the psychological phenomena the grid is intended to record, but differences in such respects do not generate any grids that cannot be analysed.

Slater goes on to define the essential properties of the grid as follows:

> A grid may be said to have certain essential properties: notably that the variation it records is due to construct–element interactions; that it defines by column a dispersion of constructs in an element space, and by row a dispersion of elements in a construct space; that the whole of the variation is restricted to a limited number of independent components, which can be ordered in magnitude from largest to least; and that each component refers both to an axis in the element space and to a corresponding axis in the construct space. In terms of these properties, a systematic, exhaustive analysis can be made of the grid.

The main output of the standard Ingrid analysis is concerned: (1) with the relationship between elements; that is to say, how similar or different are any two elements in terms of their ratings on all the constructs. This is expressed as element distances; (2) with the relationships between constructs expressed as correlations; this indicates how far one construct tends to 'go with' another in the sense that elements rated high on one tend to be rated high on the other; (3) with the underlying components of the variation in construct–element interaction. These components, which are mathematical abstractions, are axes referable both to the element space and the construct space. These will now be considered in more detail.

Relations between Elements

Two elements receiving precisely the same rating on every construct must be perceived by the subject as identical or at least indistinguishable in terms of the constructs used. Conversely, two elements rated at opposite extremes on each construct must be regarded as highly dissimilar. Overall similarity of any two elements is indicated by a measure of distance which indicates where, between these two extremes, any two elements lie in relation to each other, taking into account the degree to which they are rated similarly or differently on all the constructs used in the test. In the Ingrid program, the value for this distance between elements is calculated in such a way that two elements drawn at random from a grid of the same size would have a distance apart of 1. Element distances of less than 1 indicate that the subject sees the two elements as relatively similar, while distances of more than 1 indicate that they are relatively dissimilar. The overall similarity of any two elements in a grid can be obtained from the table of element distances in the Ingrid printout. Values for the distances between elements have a lower limit of 0 and an upper limit of the square root of $N - 1$ where $N =$ the number of

Table 5.1 Table of element distances

	SQUIRE	OFFICER	COAL-OWNER
CURATE	0.787	0.832	1.095
SQUIRE	—	1.220	0.416
OFFICER	—	—	1.352

elements in the grid. An analysis of a large number of grids reported in 'Notes on Ingrid 72' showed that the distribution of values of element distances was virtually a normal one with a mean of just below 1. In the fictitious grid of our heroine in the last chapter, the element distance table is given in Table 5.1. From this table, we can see, for example, how the officer is the one most dissimilar from the other elements.

Relations between Constructs

Just as element distances can be calculated by seeing how far two elements seem to be similarly or differently rated on all the constructs, so the relationship between any two constructs can be examined by seeing to what extent the ratings of all the elements on one of the constructs tend to match, or differ from, the ratings on the other construct. Thus, if, in general, elements rated high on *kindhearted* tend to be rated low on *intelligent*, then there is a negative association between these two constructs. The association between any two constructs based on their application to all the elements is given as a correlation with a value of −1 to +1 in the table of construct correlations in the Ingrid program printout. In calculating construct correlations, the variances of the constructs are first normalised. Construct relationships are also presented in the form of angular distances, which may be more convenient for some calculations—for example, values of angular distances can be averaged or added and subtracted when comparing grids. Angular distances run from 0 which equals a correlation of + 1, i.e. total similarity, to 90° which equals a correlation of 0, i.e. no relationship, to 180° which equals a correlation of −1, that is to say, opposite in sense.

Provided a reasonably large number of elements have been rated against the constructs, these correlations between constructs provide an indication of the underlying assumptions upon which the subject makes sense of his world of other people. Knowledge of these values can, therefore, help the tester to predict the subject's likely behaviour or to explain reported behaviour. For example, the experiences of a subject for whom the constructs *sexually attractive* and *ruthless* are positively correlated are likely to differ from those of a subject for whom these constructs are negatively correlated. The construct correlations in our fictitious heroine's grid are provided in Table 5.2. This table shows us, for example, that to be *admirable* and to be *young* are closely

Table 5.2   Table of construct correlations

	Admired	Religious	Wealthy	Approved of by mama
Youthful	0.943	0.058	−0.974	−1.000
Admired	—	−0.051	−0.962	−0.943
Religious	—	—	−0.191	−0.058
Wealthy	—	—	—	0.974

related and are linked with a perception of *maternal disapprobation*. The associations between constructs reflect general tendencies but, of course, in the case of individual elements, need not apply. Thus, a given element could be rated high on *intelligent* and low on *wise*, even if these two constructs were positively correlated in the grid as a whole.

The Principal Component Analysis

The construct correlations and element distances discussed so far represent associations between constructs which are located in mathematical terms in a space (in which there is an axis for every element) and between elements similarly located in a space (in which there is an axis for every construct). These two models of the construct–element interaction represent two views of the same data. The principal component analysis provides a common system for expressing these two dispersions. The principal component analysis extracts successive components—the first being that able to account for the most variation, the second being that accounting for the most residual variation and so on. Each component is defined by the latent root, the construct vector and the element vector from which can be derived loadings for each construct and for each element on each component.

The psychological interest of the principal component analysis is that, by identifying the systematic connections between elements and constructs in the grid, it reveals how a large number of individual judgments made by the subject in rating all the elements on all the constructs are manifestations of a relatively more simple underlying structure, and it shows which element contrasts in terms of which constructs are of major importance in the subject's system.

In most grids, the first principal component accounts for between 30 and 50 % of total variance, the second for 10 to 25 % and subsequent components for diminishing proportions.* While a component accounting for a relatively small percentage of total variance may be of psychological interest, for most practical purposes, the first two or three components provide an adequately complete picture of the subject's system.

It is usually helpful to display these components in the form of a graph or map (the old distinction between Geography as being about maps, and Psychology about chaps is no longer valid), and these maps may summarise, in the same diagram, both construct and element relations. The simplest form of display is the two-component graph. To construct one of these it is conventional to represent the first principal component by the horizontal axis and the second by the vertical axis. If these axes are drawn on a sheet of graph paper, intersecting in the middle, then each construct and each element can be located according to their loadings on these first two components. To reduce confusion and clutter in such a graph, it is better to label the elements at the point indicated by their loadings, but to label the constructs at the periphery of the graph by drawing an imaginary line out from the centre of the graph where the component axes intersect, through the point indicated by the construct loadings and extending this to the periphery. The actual loading of the constructs may be indicated by a numbered point on the graph or it may be preferable simply to exclude those constructs with loadings on both components below a certain value and to label all the remainder at the periphery. To illustrate this plotting, we can go back again to our concocted grid and express our hypothetical heroine's view of the eligible men in her circle in the form of the two-component graph (Fig. 5.1).

In summary, then, the two-component graph offers, as is apparent from this example, a geographical version of a simplified representation of conceptual space, in which the meaning of each region is indicated by the constructs and the location of each element in relation to these constructs and in relation to other elements is represented, and in which, crudely, conceptual distance is expressed as geographical distance.

A more elaborate geographical representation, taking account

* P. Slater has developed a program (GRANNY) which generates random grids, against which the variance of a given grid can be contrasted.

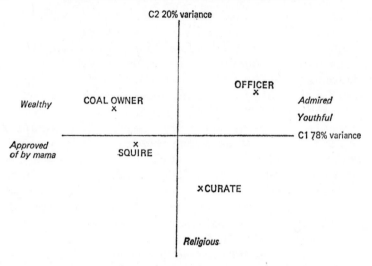

Fig. 5.1 Example of plotting two-component graph

of the first three principal components, is possible from the Ingrid program which provides data in the form of polar co-ordinates. This allows plotting on to the surface of a sphere, or on to a flat projection of a sphere (see Slater's 'Composite Diagrams and Systems of Angular Relationships Applying to Grids').

It seems reasonable to interpret grid data on the assumption that the major discriminations between elements and constructs implied by the principal components are a reflection of important psychological discriminations, hence study of spatial relationships on the two- or three-component graph enables the observer to identify the subject's crucial preoccupations and possibilities. From Fig. 5.1, for example, it can be deduced that our heroine is concerned, above all, with the differences between the officer and the other men, which in her terms appears as a contrast between admired youth and maternally approved wealth.

The Ingrid analysis is used in its normal form to process the dyad grid. In displaying the results, however, on the two-component graph, interpretation is aided if the reciprocal elements (i.e. heroine-to-officer and officer-to-heroine) are joined by a line —the dyad line. Where such lines appear in a similar area of the graph and are parallel to one another, one may assume that the reciprocal role relationships in the two pairs are construed as being similar.

Other Grid Measures

Constructs vary in the degree to which they are used by subjects to discriminate between elements, and the percentage of all the variance that is accounted for by each individual construct is provided in the grid printout. The expected percentage of variance if all constructs were of equal power can be calculated by dividing the number of constructs used into a hundred. Constructs which account for a higher proportion of variance may be described as of high salience and may be psychologically more significant. This finding could, however, be the result of incautious use of a construct which could not be used other than dichotomously; for example, *one-eyed versus two-eyed*, and the tester should be careful to avoid such constructs during test construction. The significance of the fact that a construct accounts for relatively little variation is less certain. It may be the case that the construct is usable but not very important, or it may be the case that the construct is one which the subject finds he cannot apply easily to all the elements in his test, so he may use many intermediate ratings or rate all elements similarly. This latter point should be excluded as far as possible during test construction, but as an extra precaution it is possible to allow the subject to identify on the grid any construct which he finds unable to apply to given elements by including a *not-applicable* rating. If this is done, constructs rated as *not-applicable* to more than one or two elements can be excluded from the analysis. There is another possible explanation for constructs having a low variance; it seems that constructs relating to areas of anxiety are sometimes used in a non-discriminating way, indicating the possible operation of denial mechanisms, and this point is discussed later.

The percentage of total variance accounted for by each element is listed in precisely the same way as for the constructs. This allows one to identify which elements occupy important or extreme positions in the subject's construct system.

Comparisons between Repertory Grids

It is often of interest to compare two grids. Most commonly, these will be two grids completed by the same subject on different occasions. The simplest way to compare grids is by direct comparison of selected measures such as construct correlations or element distances, or by inspection of the two-component graph.

This can tell us whether the principal components are the same on the two occasions and whether elements are distributed in the same areas and have the same relationships with each other. This procedure, however, is time-consuming and approximate and the Delta program available from the M.R.C. Unit is a valuable tool. This program is designed to compare two grids using identical constructs and elements, and produces a principal component analysis of change between the two grids. The loadings of the constructs and elements on the principal component of change provide an indication of which areas of the construct system have been most, and which least unstable. The location of change is identified, therefore, in terms both of elements and of constructs. In addition, the program provides a measure of overall similarity between two grids—the Index of General Consistency, with a value of between −1 and +1.

An unavoidable limitation in the use of the Delta program is the requirement that elements and constructs must be identical in the two tests. Clearly, the longer the interval between tests, the more likely it is that one aspect of important change may be the acquisition of new significant people and possibly of new constructs. This is especially so in subjects undergoing a radically new experience such as professional training, leaving prison, joining the army; and the same can be true of those escaping, in treatment, from the self-isolating prisons of neurotic and personality disorders. Whether, in such cases, the test grid should take in new elements and new constructs must depend upon the use to be made of the data. One practical solution would be to allow additions to the second grid, but also to preserve the original elements and constructs; one could then confine the Delta analysis of the two grids to the original construct/element list, giving the complete new grid, in addition, a separate analysis. Another solution is to use the Coin, or New Coin, program, also provided by the M.R.C. Unit. This programme compares construct relationships in two grids, using the same constructs but different elements.

The Reliability of Repertory Grid Testing and Measures of Consistency

Kelly rejected the concept of reliability and preferred to think in terms of consistency. His rejection was based upon an awareness that an apparent low reliability in a test may represent sensitivity to fluctuations in the function being measured, and his own interest was in these fluctuations. This lack of concern with reliability seems to be general in subsequent writings in Kelly's tradition, and it is chastening to discover, in writing this section, that the simplest method of testing the reliability of the method, namely short-term re-testing under identical conditions with an identical test, has seldom been reported. Bonarius (1965), in an early review of work using forms of repertory grid testing, reported a number of studies showing test/re-test correlations in the range of 0.7 to 0.8.

Measures of consistency have attracted a good deal of attention. If constructs are systematically related, then their interrelationships should be maintained when they are applied to different element pools. To the extent that these relationships differ, there must be either test error, a significant difference in the two element pools, or the subject must have an inconsistent construct system. Bannister (1962) described a consistency score, based upon the similarity of construct relationships between two grids, made up of ratings of two sets of photographs of people rated against the same set of constructs. In a further discussion of this measure (Bannister & Fransella 1966) the test was modified, in that the same set of photographs were used on both testing occasions; in this form, this test represents a short-term test/re-test measure. The consistency score derived from this test, whether the elements were the same or different photographs, has been shown to differ significantly between normals and thought-disorder schizophrenics. Frith & Lillie (1972) showed a similar relationship between thought disorder and element consistency, but these and other authors argue that the relationship between these measures and clinically diagnosed thought disorder may not be the direct one which Bannister supposes. In any case, Bannister's work showed that, in this form of test, using simple constructs applied to photographs, normals achieved high levels of test/re-test consistency (0.80).

Slater's (1972) Coin and New Coin program, which compare two grids with the same constructs but different elements, yield a measure closely similar to Bannister's consistency score, called the coefficient of convergence. Using this program, we have examined the consistency of construct relationships in two halves of the grid. The elements rated by a subject are randomly divided into two groups and these two resulting grids are compared on the Coin program. Splitting 10 grids of 12 constructs and 24 elements yielded values for the coefficient of convergence between 0.277 and 0.713 (median value over 0.5). Long-term re-test studies, designed to measure function fluctuation—i.e. change in the construct structure and element relationships—will be discussed in later chapters.

Validity

Validation of test measures requires the existence of independent criteria for measuring the function assessed. In the case of the repertory grid technique, an extensive range of data is available and is open to interpretation in a number of ways and the technique itself may be employed for a variety of purposes. There is, therefore, no general validation available for the method. In a later chapter, two validation studies of repertory grid technique as a means of identifying neurotics from normals are described.

List of publications from the Medical Research Council Unit for the processing of repertory grids, obtainable from the Unit at the Institute of Psychiatry, De Crespigny Park, Denmark Hill, London S.E. 5:

Notes on Ingrid 67
Advice on Submitting Grids for Analysis on Ingrid 67
A Summary of the Output from Delta
Notes on Ingrid 72
Composite Diagrams and Systems of Angular Relationships Applying to Grids

The Ingrid and Delta series of programs, written by Patrick Slater of the M.R.C. Unit, for analysing repertory grids, are available via the 7600 link from various universities in Britain. These connect to the London University computer. The programs are called up as files stored in U.L.C.C., and turn-around time for analysis is between two days and two weeks.

6

Interpretation of Test Results

Views of the SELF and SIGNIFICANT OTHERS

At its simplest, the repertory grid provides the subject with an opportunity for self-description. By including the SELF as one of a range of elements rather than by rating the SELF against a range of descriptions, the tendency for bias to influence the self-rating is probably diminished; it is easier to describe ONESELF as *less intelligent* than EINSTEIN or *more selfish* than one's WIFE than it is to give ONESELF a low rating on a scale measuring *intelligence* or a high rating on a scale measuring *selfishness*. While the possibility of presenting a view of the SELF which is distorted by defensiveness or by the wish to please cannot be ruled out, the fact that the subject co-operates in the creation of the test is probably helpful in diminishing this tendency. If the tester undertakes to feed back the results of the test to the subject (and unless this interferes with some research design this seems a reasonable thing to do), then conscious distortions of the self-image presented are unlikely to occur.

The Location of the SELF on the Two-Component Graph

The two-component graph of the RG test provides the most accessible evidence about the self-concept, allowing one to see in which area of the map the SELF is located and in what company. As an example, let us look at the test of a very anxious student who was finding it difficult to settle down in the University and who eventually withdrew after a period of increasing social isolation and some episodes of self-injury (Fig. 6.1). (In this and subsequent examples, a simplified two-component graph is presented, omitting those constructs with low loadings on the components and not plotting the construct numbers on the graph. The percentage variance accounted for by each component is indicated. The sex of elements is indicated by o = female, x = male.)

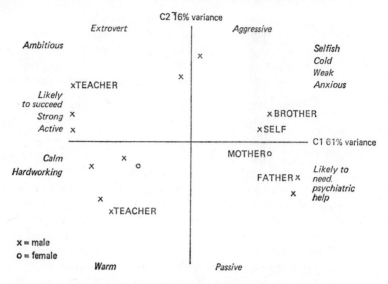

Fig. 6.1 Two-component graph

This test shows someone who sees the world in stark black and white terms as being made up on the one hand of his family, characterised by all the negative qualities, and on the other hand by everyone else. This student's depression also found expression in his inability to rate the element YOURSELF AS YOU WOULD LIKE TO BE.

Relation of SELF to IDEAL SELF

The inclusion of the IDEAL SELF as an element on the grid provides some indication of the degree of dissatisfaction with the SELF and of the nature of the deficiency perceived. It is characteristic of neurotic patients to have a large SELF/IDEAL SELF discrepancy, and indeed without such discrepancy the motivation for treatment is dubious. Ideal figure elements of any sort tend to be extremely rated and hence to appear with high loadings on the principal components. In the course of treatment the SELF/IDEAL SELF separation may increase as defences are removed, and then come closer as self-dissatisfaction decreases. In some cases, this approximation may reflect a revision of the ideal away from unrealistic expectations, while in others the SELF may be seen to shift nearer to an ideal which is still seen as desirable. Two examples are given. Fig. 6.2 is the graph of a male

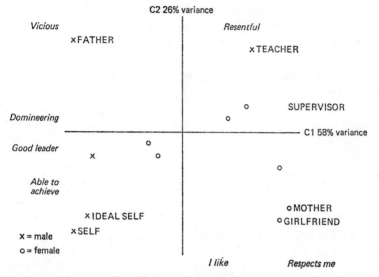

Fig. 6.2 Two-component graph

student who displayed aggressive, antisocial behaviour and who also failed academically. The SELF is contrasted favourably with the MOTHER and GIRL-FRIEND on the first component, and with the FATHER on the second, and the IDEAL SELF is located very

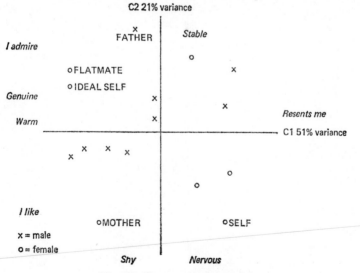

Fig. 6.3 Two-component graph

FG—D

close to the SELF. This student did not accept treatment and left the University after academic and disciplinary problems. Fig. 6.3 is the graph of a female student who consulted with depression and relationship problems. Here the IDEAL SELF is vastly different from the negatively rated SELF, and closely resembles the FLATMATE. This girl did not persist with therapy, but over the next two years moved, as far as could be judged from brief occasional contacts, to much greater self-acceptance; unfortunately, she refused to complete a re-test. Incidentally, the idealised flatmate subsequently required psychotherapy.

Relation of SELF to Identification Models

Differing theories of identification converge at least to the point of agreeing that the individual's sex role learning owes much to the roles played by his mother and father. While most research points to the fact that children of either sex identify with both their parents, there is reasonably good evidence that strong identification with a parent of the opposite sex is liable to cause difficulty. Some of the research data in this area are summarised in a paper describing a repertory grid study of identification (Ryle & Lunghi 1972).

In inspecting the two-component graph of a standard grid, the

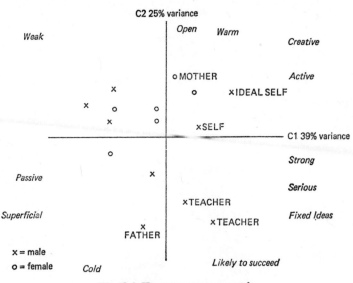

Fig. 6.4 Two-component graph

position of SELF and IDEAL SELF in relation to both PARENTS may provide indications of identification phenomena. As an example, Fig. 6.4 is the two-component graph of a male student who was successful academically despite a severe speech impediment and tic. At a psychiatric assessment interview, he described a conflict he recognised in himself between the striving, high-achieving SELF, and a suppressed part which was manifest in an elaborate fantasy about being an itinerant painter or singer. This conflict appears on the graph as the choice between cold success (like father) or warm creativity (like mother). In this case, preserving a male self-concept may have involved the denial or suppression of aspects of the self.

Studies of identification have usually been based upon measures of perceived similarity between SELF and model, but in many ways it may be more appropriate to think in terms of resemblance in respect of reciprocal roles, and the dyad grid may give more direct evidence of this type of similarity. In plotting the two-component graph for a dyad grid, the two elements of each dyad are joined by a line—the dyad line. When two dyad lines are parallel one may deduce that the perceived reciprocal roles of the two pairs are seen as similar. The relation between SELF and SPOUSE, SELF and PARENT, and PARENT and PARENT is of

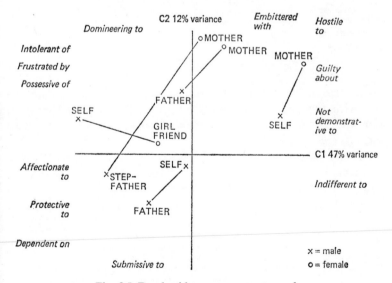

Fig. 6.5 Dyad grid two-component graph

prime interest. An example of a two-component graph with these pairs, in which the relationship of MOTHER-to-STEPFATHER is also included, is given in Fig. 6.5. This is the case of a male post-graduate student whose parents had divorced when he was thirteen. The dyad grid graph shows a MOTHER who is seen as *powerful* and *destructive* to FATHER, STEPFATHER and self, the male role being *submissive* and *dependent*. This student consulted with depression, self-violence and a difficult relationship with a

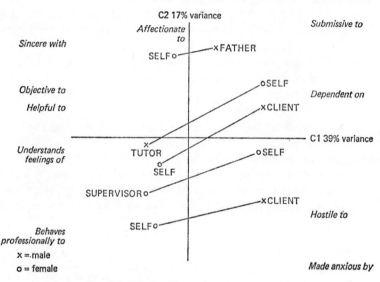

Fig. 6.6 Dyad grid two-component graph

frigid, dependent girl-friend. The graph shows how the relation-ship with the girl-friend partially repeats the maternal pattern, with the SELF seen as being *more attracted, possessive, demanding* and *affectionate than* the GIRL.

Parents, of course, are not the only identification figures, and an example is given in Fig. 6.6. of a dyad grid of a social work student in which the importance of the TUTOR-to-STUDENT and SUPERVISOR-to-STUDENT interaction as providing role models for the social work STUDENT-to-CLIENT relationship is apparent.

The SELF in Different Roles

STANDARD GRID

The use of the standard grid with multiple definitions of the

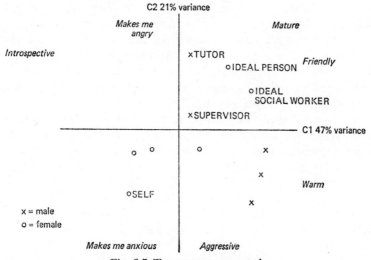

Fig. 6.7 Two-component graph

SELF provides one way of investigating how far the subject sees himself as consistent or differentiated in his different roles.

As an example, this approach has been used in investigation of social work students in training. In this study, (initiated by

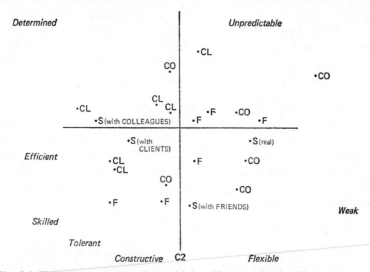

Fig. 6.8 Two-component graph: multiple-self-as-perceived grid
Versions of the SELF: CO = as seen by COLLEAGUES; CL = as seen by CLIENTS; F = as seen by FRIENDS; S = as seen by SELF

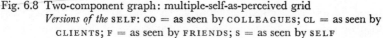

M. Lunghi), the SELF and two IDEAL SELVES were incorpor-
ated (the PERSON YOU WOULD LIKE TO BE, and the SOCIAL
WORKER YOU WOULD LIKE TO BE), to see whether the two
ideals were in any way in conflict. An example from this study is
given in Fig. 6.7, in which the IDEAL FIGURES are seen to be
close together and in which TUTORS and SUPERVISORS again
seem to provide (as in Fig. 6.6) role models.

In a similar study of trained social workers (carried out by
R. R. Ryle and J. Mulvey) this approach was modified in that
subjects were asked to rate themselves as they believed they were
seen by members of three different groups of others, namely
clients, colleagues and friends, and also as they felt they really
were (The Multiple-Self-as-Perceived-Grid). Fig. 6.8 is an example from this study. There is a considerable degree of segrega-
tion of the different versions of the SELF.

SIGNIFICANT OTHERS

In the above examples, SIGNIFICANT OTHERS have figured
(1) as identification models who may be seen as similar to or
different from the SUBJECT; (2) as perceivers of the SUBJECT in
the Multiple-Self-as-Perceived version of the standard grid; and
(3) at the reciprocal pole to the SELF of dyad lines in the dyad
grid. There is one other way in which they may be interpreted,
namely as representing projected or lost parts of the SELF.
Discussion of this aspect of the SIGNIFICANT OTHER, however,
will be deferred to the next chapter when evidence of possible
unconscious factors will be considered.

Options

The analysis of the grid offered so far has been an essentially
static one. To complement this approach, we will now discuss
how one can look at the ways in which the nature of the subject's
construct space and the distribution of elements in it can be
interpreted as defining his options and limiting or determining
his future possibilities.

CONSTRUCT CORRELATIONS

The first evidence one can draw upon in seeking to define the
subject's options is the table of construct correlations. As this is a
large table one would normally, in clinical work with grids,
sample this according to some preconception of one's own, or by

inspecting only the correlations of those constructs most salient to the subject, i.e. those accounting for the highest percentage of variance. For example, in a study of couples, clinical interest might focus on the construct *sexually attracted to*, while in a study of students failing in academic work, the construct *likely to succeed academically* might be of particular interest.

The sense to be made from these construct correlations is largely common sense. Let us consider four examples.

1. If a girl with a history of repeated disastrous sexual relationships produces a grid in which the construct *is sexually attracted to me* has a strong negative correlation with the construct *a thoughtful and reliable person*, one can understand her history better and one must predict a repetition of the disasters unless this association is altered.

2. If the grid of a bright but academically failing female student contains a negative correlation between the constructs *academically able* and *feminine*, one can understand the implicit cost of success to her, and the grid has helped to locate the conflict underlying her failure.

3. If a bright, but academically failing male student produces a grid in which constructs such as *effective person, masculine* or *strong character* have negative correlations with the construct *resembles me in character*, while constructs like *sensitive* or *artistic* or *kind* have positive correlations with *resembles me*, then the subject would seem to be unable to identify himself with any of the conventional male attributes. In such a case, the academic difficulty would probably represent a passive/aggressive response to authority, and an underlying homosexual problem might be suspected.

4. If, in the grid of a social work student, the construct *makes me angry* and the construct *dependent upon me* are highly correlated, one would predict difficulties in casework relationships with dependent clients which would need careful supervision and working through.

These four examples are readily comprehensible in terms of common sense, but common sense can, of course, be a self-deceiving label for the tester's preconceptions and the 'correct' or 'healthy' value for a correlation between any given pair of constructs might be defined by a number of conflicting criteria. This raises the whole issue of the relationship between truth and consensus and between the various definitions of normal. In practice one can avoid these thorny problems in interpreting a given grid by refraining from normative comments of any kind. To take the second example above, whether or not society at large or most girls regard achievement as unfeminine is irrelevant; this girl, in her own terms, does so, and before she can be both a woman and successful she has to resolve this conflict.

While the individual's own construct relationships must always be the best guide to understanding him, the relation of his structure of meaning to that of others is also of interest. For some purposes, therefore, there may be a value in establishing the range and distribution of the values of certain construct correlations within a given population. This can be done in group studies in which some common supplied constructs are included in the test. Examples of these will be given later in the book. In these cases, the values for each individual for correlations between supplied constructs can be identified as low, median or high in relation to this given group. On this basis one may be able to predict, with more confidence, how this individual's experience will differ from that of the rest of the group. For example, a social work student for whom dependence is annoying will have different problems from one for whom it is gratifying; in a grid where elements are clients, this difference in the implications of dependency could be detected from the correlations between constructs such as *depends on me, makes me angry* and *I enjoy caring for*.

In summary, the conclusions deduced from construct correlations may be formulated in the following manner: 'within this system the subject cannot see the possibility of being both A and B, or he cannot be C without also being D.' (For example, he cannot be both strong and gentle, or he cannot be sexually potent without also being destructive.)

ELEMENT DISTRIBUTION ON THE TWO-COMPONENT GRAPH

Dilemmas facing a subject may be manifest through the position of the SELF in relation to ROLE MODELS or IDEAL FIGURES on the two-component graph. If one looks at a two-component graph as a map of territory through which the SELF could move, one can see how movement in any given direction involves entering space defined by the construct loadings on the components and by the other elements located in it; that is to say,

it involves him in accepting certain self-attributions and similarities to certain others. An example was provided above (Fig.
6.4) of a student with a speech problem and a tic, who balanced
devotion to academic work with an unrealistic fantasy of living an
artistic life for which he was not equipped. The two-component
graph illustrated this dilemma both in terms of which parent he
might wish to resemble and which qualities he might aspire to.

From the above discussion it is clear that, for a given individual,
the possibility of change can be defined in grid terms in two ways.
On the one hand, his options may be extended by movement
within his existing construct space, and on the other hand, he may
modify this space so that the construct correlations and principal
components of the system are altered.

7

The Interpretation of
Repertory Grid Test Results in the
Light of Psychoanalytic Theory

The Attitude of Personal Construct
Theorists to Psychoanalysis

Kelly, like most innovators, had the defects of his qualities, and along with his exuberant affirmation of the philosophical stance of constructive alternativism and his energetic attempt to create a truly comprehensive psychological theory, went a propensity for intolerant caricature of alternative theories. Holland (1970) spells out Kelly's cavalier dismissal of Freud and his failure to relate, in a remotely adequate way, his own position to that of psychoanalysis. What may be excusable in a prophet is harder to forgive in a disciple, yet we find a similar vein of dismissive propagandist argument in the most recent exposition of personal construct theory, *Inquiring Man* by Bannister & Fransella (1971). These authors refer to the 'Freudian portrait of man as essentially infantile, trapped in his own inadequate attempts to deal with his sexual, aggressive, destructive, death-seeking powers . . .', and write of psychoanalysis that the doctor insists that he 'comprehends the mysteries, he is the expert, he possesses the skill, the "patient" is ill and hopes, through the intervention of the doctor, to become well'. Yet, the most superficial acquaintance with the psychoanalytic writing of the last forty years will show the central importance accorded in the development of theory and in the practice of therapy to the patient's ego functions and to the need for the analyst to reject the priest-like role patients may invest him with.

Personal construct theory emphasises the need to construe the construction processes of the other, implicitly warns against the temptation of the false dichotomy, and in its formal structure recognises the possibility of alternative constructions of the same event. It demonstrates how theories, besides competing, or over-lapping, may be usefully distinguished as having different fields of relevance. That, despite this, adherents of personal construct theory display postures of such ungenerous incomprehension, suggests that there may be a need for a construct like 'the unconscious'.

My own use of the repertory grid technique has been in investigating interpersonal processes, especially psychotherapy. In many cases, I have been involved clinically, as a psychotherapist, while simultaneously seeking to understand what was going on in terms of personal construct and object-relations theory. For this reason, the overlaps, convergences, equivalences, and uniqueness of the two accounts have been a central interest. In this chapter, some provisional conclusions drawn from this approach are offered. Before this, however, a brief account of what I mean by psychoanalytic theory is necessary.

The Evolution of Psychoanalytic Theory

The first thing to say about psychoanalytic theory is that it is not a single coherent body of theory so much as an evolving, untidy and often impenetrable confusion of theories. Within this confusion, however, is one distinguishing thread which, in my view, represents the main creative impact of psychoanalysis on psychology. This is the attempt to understand the experience and behaviour of the adult by reference to early, especially infantile, experience. This attempt involves, inevitably, the exploration of times not recorded in coherent thought, and not to be construed through ordinary adult conceptions; to give an account of these times is, essentially, an exercise in decoding symbols and in model-building. As the experiences being construed are chaotic, highly charged with feeling and not available to experimental manipulation, it is not surprising that the models offered within psychoanalysis are often inadequate and have undergone constant revision and change.

Freud's own thinking was marked by continual re-formulation rather than by any tendency towards orthodoxy, and the development of psychoanalytic thought has been marked by diversification, even if sterile orthodoxies and factional struggles have marked many of its chapters. This evolution has been characterised by a progressive move away from biological or physical science models of psychic functioning, towards social models, and by a move away from an emphasis on structural and energy concepts to emphasis on ego functions and on the central significance of the self. This progress is well summarised in Guntrip (1971) and the latter author's writings represent the version of object-relations theory which I personally find the most satisfying.

An Outline of the Object-Relations Theory of Infantile Development

In Guntrip's view, the development of the individual is best described as the growth of the self in a social context, a growth characterised by a basic object-seeking quality; that is to say, by a search to relate to others, which is present in all human infants. This search for the other, and through the other, the discovery of the self, goes through the early vicissitudes described by Klein (1948, 1957) and extended by Fairbairn (1952). In the early months of the infant's life, the most basic assumptions about the self are formed—those to do with the boundaries between the self and not-self, and with the relationship of, and distinction between, inner and outer reality. These are developed through the infant's groping understanding of what is inside and outside the body, and worked at by way of preoccupations with the orifices which connect the inside and outside. These orifices are important symbolic channels of communication in the child's earliest relationships. Disturbances in these early stages, it is postulated, are manifest in the schizoid states, where the self is felt to be so feeble that it must be hidden, or so ill-bounded that it is at constant risk of invasion by the other, and in the paranoid states, whereby inner and outer reality and the boundaries of the self from the other are so unclearly differentiated that, in fantasy, the inner processes can control the outer world or the outer world can control or invade the inner. The threats and dangers of these fantasies are dealt with by the mechanisms of projection and introjection, expressed symbolically through the mouth and anus, whereby the good in others is symbolically taken into the self, and the dangerous destructiveness in the self is projected into the other. These mechanisms can, in fantasy, lead to the further danger of exhausting the other of all resource, or overwhelming him, or of filling the other with the projected primitive destructive force and then being threatened by this force. Envy is born at this stage out of the relatively powerless infant's need to depend upon the relatively resourceful mother.

Faced with a mother who is powerful and envied, and into whom the infant's own destructiveness may be projected, and also with a mother who is dependable and, indeed, indispensable, the infant may seek to conserve and idealise the relationship of good mother-to-contended baby by splitting off, in fantasy, a separate bad mother-to-destructive baby relationship. This process is the origin of discrimination but, if retained in this crude form, provides the basis for part object-relationships identified in later life. In these, the individual seeks to reconstitute the pattern laid down by the early split, with the self variably deployed in the roles of needy baby, destructive baby, good mother, or depriving, attacking mother, and the other selected or induced to fulfil the appropriate reciprocal role. Out of this inner drama between part objects, comes the neurotic repetition-compulsion in which a series of stereotypic 'bit parts' are played over and over again, reflecting the primitive patterning of split relationships in his inner world.

To grow from his early split relationship with the mother, the infant must abandon the fantasy of the ever-present good mother, and accept the mixed feelings implicit in this abandonment. Through his recognition of his mother's separateness, he also achieves his own separation; this is the depressive position as described by Klein. In its healthy evolution, it is marked by the dawn of the wish to repair in fantasy the harm done, out of which grows the adult capacity for concern.

In the next stage, the child becomes more concerned with power and with the gradual acquisition of autonomy, and hence with rivalry, especially with the parent of the same sex for the parent of the opposite sex, and with siblings for the care and attention of the parents. To the extent that the parents can maintain their own appropriate separation from their children and their own united, adult relationship with each other, the child can develop in this process a clearer concept of himself, a more elaborate construct of his role—including his sex role—and a new form of autonomy which includes the taking on of responsibility for his own social behaviour; that is to say, the child begins to look after and control himself. To the extent that early processes have not been fully resolved, and to the extent, therefore, that the boundaries of the self and the symbolisation of the relationships of self to other through the orifices (mouth, excretory, genital) are incompletely resolved, the later incorporation of sex identity and of responsible social control may be tied up with split or part object versions of self-to-other relationships and with primitive, destructive forces. Against these dangers, the defences of denial, repression and dissociation come into play.

Object-Relations Theory and Psychotherapy

This object-relations account of infantile development can be regarded as a fairy tale, albeit as a rather brutal one. It is an attempt to give an account, in adult words and concepts, of what may happen in infancy, an account designed to explain adult experience and behaviour. What is the relation of this account to psychoanalytically based psychotherapy? Between the hypothesised infant experience and the adult neurosis is a screen of forgetfulness, and for each individual patient in therapy, the attempt must be made to identify what remainders or reminders of early experience are still active in determining his view of himself and others, his expectations and his assumptions and his fantasies about what is possible or what may be the consequences of particular actions. In addition, in therapy, the defences he employs to avoid or contain the forces in both the outer and inner world must be recognised. In so far as these traces, or unconscious forces, are only accessible or relevant through their effect upon present here-and-now experience, the exactness of the fairy tale is not crucial. What is crucial is that the model can enable the therapist to recognise what the patient means and what he means to the patient, and to convey this recognition in his words and behaviour to the patient. The modification of unconscious, infantile constructs commences with this recognition, but involves, of course, much more than understanding and communicating. The question to be considered here, however, is how far repertory grid data may confirm or contribute to this kind of understanding, and how far psychoanalytic theory may be used to make sense of the grids produced by patients.

Indications of Unconscious Mental Processes

Before discussing what inferences the tester may draw about possible unconscious processes from repertory grid data, it is worth considering how far the subject may reveal, through his conscious verbal task of completing the grid test, information which, when processed and fed back to him, can be in some sense unfamiliar or unknown. Evidence here is essentially anecdotal;

anybody who has discussed with subjects the results of analysing their repertory grid data will, I believe, have had the experience of seeing the subject becoming aware of aspects of himself which, partially or wholly, he did not recognise and could not have formulated before. A subject's response to feedback of this sort can be very similar to the response sometimes made by a patient to an interpretation in psychotherapy. Sometimes the subject exper-iences something 'clicking' which makes obvious and valuable sense to him. Sometimes his response is one of disbelief or evasion, though this is hard to sustain in so far as the repertory grid test is the subject's own work and in his own language (except on those embarrassing occasions when the tester has made some mistake in the coding or display of the grid data). At other times, the subject may offer correction, clarification or development of the tester's formulation. The subject's ability to grasp what the test shows about his psychological processes does not, of course, necessarily enable him to change them, for insight alone seldom can produce change; but the knowledge derived from the test may enable him to see more clearly the possibility of alternative constructions of the world. In any case, grid data can enable subject and tester, or patient and therapist to explore together and develop alternative and clearer formulations about what is known or half known. To take a concrete example, let us say that one confronts a subject with the fact that, on the basis of the construct correlations of his grid, it seems as if he identifies *potency* with *destructiveness*; and that, on the basis of the two-component graph, it appears that he identifies with the PARENT and the elements of the opposite sex and that it seems, in his terms, impossible to be in the more *potent* area of the construct space without abandoning *expressiveness* or *sensitivity*. Such a subject is exhibiting a fairly common form of uncertainty about sex role; but in restating the problem in these terms, he may be faced with things which he only half suspected or half understood before. In doing this, one seems to me to be carrying out a process indistinguishable from that aspect of psychotherapeutic interpretation which is concerned with 'making the unconscious conscious' and its seems legitimate to say, there-fore, that repertory grid testing is providing access to unconscious mental processes. We will now proceed to study ways in which particular unconscious mechanisms may be manifest in grid data.

Ambivalence, Splitting, Projection and Introjection

Ambivalence is defined as a conscious awareness of mixed, opposing feelings for another. Evidence of it can be obtained from grid data by asking the subject to rate the same elements twice as experienced under different conditions. In the dyad grid, for example, the subject can rate his relationship with a significant other and the other's relationship to the self when they are sad or when they are happy, or when the relationship is going well and when it is going badly. Looked for, in this way, on the dyad grid, major distinctions between the two conditions are often revealed on the two-component graph. Usually, as would be expected, the main difference is a shift of the dyad along the component on which the positive and negative evaluative constructs have their highest loadings. In the twenty or so cases tested personally in this way, this shift has never been accompanied by any alteration in the reciprocal roles of the pair between the two conditions; but the length of the dyad line is nearly always greater under the 'going badly' condition of the relationship, indicating that when negative feeling is predominant, there is greater differentiation perceived in the reciprocal roles.

Serial testing, by a rating of the same relationship on successive occasions through time, represents another technique for recording variations in mutual construing, through which ambivalence might well become apparent through fluctuations in construing, although so far, I have only very limited experience of this technique.

In the case of splitting, the subject 'resolves' ambivalence, or avoids facing it, by segregating the opposing qualities between different subjects. An analogous process is the way in which certain qualities may be taken into the self (introjection) and others put into the other (projection). Being an unconscious process and, in object-relations developmental theory, a primitive one at that, the subject cannot directly display these mechanisms to the tester. What is more, the distinction between splitting mechanisms of this sort and ordinary discrimination—which, in the Kleinian view, represents the normal outcome of infantile splitting—is essentially one of degree. In the interpretation of the individual grid, it is, in my view, always worth considering the possibility of splitting mechanisms where the self or key others have a very high loading on one of the principal components. In such a case, the space on the two-component graph polar to the element—or the element occupying that space—may indicate a denied, split-off aspect of the element being considered. Evidence that neurotic subjects do polarise themselves and significant others significantly more than normals is presented in a later chapter.

In so far as splittings are derived from the non-resolution of the early good–bad, strong–weak splitting of the mother in relation to the infantile self, and the subsequent imposition of these part-object versions of relationships as a matrix through which current others are construed, it is clear that one can look upon the two-component graph as an indistinct, approximate guide to the subject's inner world of object-relations. To this extent, the relatively unchanging quality of this inner world, which underlies the neurotic repetition-compulsion whereby the subject repeats, over and over again, similar patterns and modes of relating, may be illuminated by study of the repertory grid.

Oedipal Patterns

Successful resolution of the oedipal conflict is achieved when the individual accepts the fact that his parents are united by a sexual relationship and when he himself has accepted the de-sexualisation of his relationship with the parent of the opposite sex; evidence of successful resolution in the adult is the ability to combine sexuality and affection in a relationship with a contemporary of the opposite sex. This resolution is usually achieved by identification with the parent of the same sex, but where this parent presents a poor role model, it may still be achieved through modelling on other figures. Possible unresolved oedipal problems may be discernible in the grid, therefore, in a number of ways. Inspection of construct correlations, or the nature of the principal components, may show that appropriate, or conventional, sex role characteristics are linked with negative or unacceptable attributes; thus masculinity may be equated with insensitivity, or femininity with weakness. On the two-component graph, the relative position of self, parents and other elements may show closeness (i.e. identification) with elements of the opposite sex, and a denial or loss of appropriate attributes for the self. On the dyad grid, the relative positions of self-to-mother, self-to-father, and self-to-sexual partner may show a repetition, with the spouse repeating the pattern shown in relation to the parent, indicating the possibility that sexual taboo will operate; or the self-to-spouse dyad line may reverse the reciprocal sex roles perceived between the parents. This latter picture may represent either a failure to follow normal role modelling, or the successful correction of a culturally deviant reversal in the parental pair.

Repression and Denial

Completing an RG test is a conscious act, and the subject obviously cannot record what is repressed or denied; but indirect evidence of the operation of these mechanisms is provided by the subject's choice, or non-choice, and use, or non-use, of constructs. As regards choice of constructs, some subjects will have great difficulty in providing constructs to do with feeling at all; others will produce only those to do with benign and positive feeling, and attempts on the part of the tester to elicit the implicit negative poles of these constructs may be evaded. Other subjects may include negatively charged constructs but in completing the test will not use them in a discriminating way. This may be particularly true in relation to sexual and angry feeling, and subjects with problems in these areas may rate all elements as equally low on aggression or sexuality. This tendency is manifest in the data output from the grid analysis in that the constructs concerned account for a very small proportion of the total variance of the grid.

Fantasy

Unconscious fantasy, in psychoanalytical terms, describes the way in which patients act as if they were still engaged in an earlier experience—an earlier experience which will itself have been based upon a primitive symbolisation or a misinterpretation of reality in some degree. Repertory grid techniques can help one understand the nature of the patient's apparent misperception of the current situation, but cannot throw light directly on the truth or otherwise of psychoanalytic theories about the origins of such misperception. Thus, a male whose RG test shows a high correlation between masculinity and cruelty, and who construes himself as gentle, passive and like his mother, will act as if to be masculine is bad or dangerous and will avoid competition with powerful men. In analytical terms such a man is manifesting castration anxiety and is behaving as if dominated by the fantasy that his male aggression or assertion is forbidden. In a general sense, the operation of fantasy may be suspected from the repertory grid wherever particular attributes are linked with others not normally so linked; or where the movement of the self in the construct space implies particular and unusual costs to the self. This suspicion is based upon the assumption that subjects operating in the same world need to operate with a more or less consensual view of it. Departure from the socially shared consensus leads to false predictions about the responses of others. There are, however, clearly areas—particularly to do with broader social rather than interpersonal issues—where to dismiss non-consensual construing as fantasy would be quite unjustified.

Resistance in Psychotherapy

The tendency of a patient in therapy to block change is one aspect of the individual's need to maintain constancy in his mode of construing the world. During periods of rapid change in therapy and under other emotionally strenuous conditions, people often experience a sense of confusion accompanied by uncertainty about reality and uncertainty about the self. It seems likely that depersonalisation and derealisation experiences, and free-floating anxiety, may represent the subject's awareness of the failure of his system to reliably construe his experience. The confusion resulting from too much loosening of construct structure may be solved by a return to a rigid, simplified structure and this tendency may represent one aspect of resistance to change in therapy. In a study of social-work students, tested before and after a T-Group experience, half the sample showed a simpler construct system, in which the first two principal components accounted for a greater proportion of total variance, following the T-Group experience; but over the whole course of two-year training, all but one of the sample showed the opposite tendency, indicating that they had learnt to view their relationships with a greater complexity (Ryle & Breen, 1974). The most important aspect of resistance to psychotherapy, however, is that related to the transference. One of the first uses made of repertory grid technique in Britain was Crisp's study of transference (1964) in which he showed how a shift in the patient's construing of his therapist, measured by a form of repertory grid testing, was systematically accompanied by changes in observed transference behaviour. However, there have been few systematic studies of transference carried out since this study. In object-relations theory terms, transference is the process whereby the patient invests the therapist with qualities derived from past, usually parental, figures; or, more precisely, derived from the internalised part object-relations with such figures. In analytically oriented psychotherapy, the recognition of the processes involved in transference, and the repeated confrontation of the patient with the therapist's refusal to collude by taking on the ascribed part object roles and attributes, is a central part of the treatment process. A problem about using grid techniques to investigate this area is posed by the phenomena of ambivalence and splitting, discussed above. A patient in therapy may experience simultaneously, or in quick succession, profoundly different feelings in relation to his therapist as the therapist becomes the focus of different part object-relations. To pick up these mixed and changing feelings by grid testing demands additional techniques or interpretations of grid data. It seems probable that the most effective means would be to use serial testing through the process of therapy, and some preliminary work along these lines has been carried out.

8

Differences between Neurotic and Normal Subjects on the RG Test

In the last chapters we have considered various ways in which RG test data may suggest how a given individual views himself and others, how his options for change may be limited, and how one may detect evidence pointing to the operation of some of the unconscious processes discussed in psychoanalytic writing. Not all the inferences made will be self-evident or acceptable to those not accepting object-relations theory, and, as my own thinking and understanding of grid data had developed largely from a simultaneous involvement with patients as a psychotherapist and as a researcher (though the actual construction and administration of the tests was carried out by my colleagues), the possibility of consistent self-deception was ever present. However, I remained personally convinced that this way of approaching grid data, while not the only one, was a valuable one capable of identifying many neurotic mechanisms. The conviction that grid features indicating neurotic processes could be identified became strong enough for me to test out the various hunches and generalisations developed along the way. Two experiments were carried out; these will be discussed in outline here, full details being given in published papers (Ryle & Breen 1971, 1972a).

In the first experiment, sixteen standard grids were presented in randomly numbered order, eight being the grids of controls (randomly selected from students who had attended a testing session and who had no history of psychiatric consultation), and eight being the grids of student psychiatric patients. To be classified as a patient, a student had consulted a doctor in the University Health Service, and had been assessed as having a problem of sufficient severity to warrant at least four long appointments. Patients identified by this operational criterion differed significantly from controls in their scores on the Middlesex Hospital Questionnaire.

The sixteen grids were presented blind and were ranked according to the probability that the subject was a psychiatric patient. This rank ordering was carried out on the basis of an inspection of the grids in which the features suggestive of neurosis described in Chapters 6 and 7 were looked for. The rank order position of each subject was then related to patient or non-patient status. It was found that the grids ranked 1–6, 8 and 10 were those of patients. On checking the medical records of the eight controls it was found that Nos. 7, 9, 11 and 12 had each consulted on one occasion with minor emotional symptoms during the fifteen months since testing. It seemed, therefore, that the range of criteria used had given a reliable indication of the presence of neurotic difficulties.

The second experiment was, in some senses, a more stringent test of the assumptions behind RG interpretations and was based upon a list of specific predictions about how a number of grid variables would differ between patients and controls defined by the same criteria as above. As an additional criterion of neurosis, the subjects also completed the Middlesex Hospital Questionnaire (Crown & Crisp 1966). While this procedure is more in the tradition of validation studies, it is to some degree loaded against the grid, as only a limited range of grid variables could be systematically compared between different grids. The grid used in the test included some supplied constructs and a standard number of elements, some with supplied role-titles. No account could be taken of the position of the elements in the construct space as each subject had a different set of constructs and elements apart from those supplied or specified. Within these limitations, which would not operate in the interpretation of a grid in the clinical situation, a number of predictions were made of differences in means and of differences in the variance of a number of grid measures in relation to patient status and M.H.Q. score.

In all, the grids of thirty-three patients and fifty-four controls were included in the study. Despite the limitations imposed by the design, this experiment also demonstrated that the interpretations made of grid measures were based upon relevant considerations, for in the majority of instances, the grid variables selected either differed between patients and controls in the direction predicted, or were correlated as predicted with the M.H.Q. scores, or were related to both patient status and M.H.Q. scores.

These findings may be summarised as follows:

1. Patients differed significantly from controls in respect of a number of measures of identification, defined as similarity of self to others and measured as element distances. Thus, among patients there was a greater separation between the self and ideal self; a greater separation between self and father; a greater mean distance between self and mother and father; and a greater relative closeness to mother compared to father. In addition, looking at the measures of element distance, patients had significantly more other elements at a distance of 1 or more from the self than did the controls.

2. Two measures suggesting the operation of splitting mechanisms and polarisation were also significantly greater among patients.

   (i) Male patients had significantly greater loadings of the self on the first and second principal components of their grids than did controls.

   (ii) In patients, a significantly greater percentage of total variance was accounted for by the first and second principal components combined than in controls. These differences indicate that patients see themselves as more extreme in respect of the main discriminations made between people than do controls, and that they judge themselves and others in a simpler, more one- or two-dimensional system, than do controls.

Correlations between summed M.H.Q. scores and the twenty-three grid measures included in the study repeated many of these findings, and in addition, (i) high M.H.Q. scores were correlated with high self–mother distance (i.e. with low identification with mother); (ii) certain construct correlations were examined and it was found that the correlations between *warm* and *passive* and between *warm* and *likely to need psychiatric help* were significantly higher with higher M.H.Q. scores. A further measure of the tendency to polarise or make extreme judgments—the mean construct variation—was also significantly correlated with high M.H.Q. scores.

The repertory grid portrait of the neurotic as opposed to the normal, which emerged from this study, was summarised in the original paper as follows:

The neurotic . . . is someone who sees himself as unlike others in general, and unlike his parents in particular; who is dissatisfied with himself; who tends to extreme judgments; and who operates with a less complex construct system than do normals; and who tends to construe others in ways which depart from consensual values in respect of certain attributes. In addition, an account of an individual patient would include a description of the particular possibilities open or closed to him on account of his mode of construing himself and others.

The finding of Adams-Webber (1969) that subjects of low cognitive complexity, measured with a form of grid testing, were less able to infer the personal constructs of others would complement this portrait of the neurotic whose characteristic failure to cope successfully with personal relationships reflects these personal construct characteristics.

This portrait cannot be taken as confirming or disconfirming any particular theory of neurosis, but, in conjunction with the preceding chapters, it suggests that the RG technique does provide evidence of explanatory and predictive potential. More important, it suggests that, in addition to the valuable ideographic emphasis of personal construct theory and of RG technique, the interpretation of test results can be based upon the recognition of certain features as indicative of psychopathology.

The dyad grid has not, so far, been validated as an indicator of neurosis in the same way as the standard grid, but a study of its use in adjusted and maladjusted couples will be reported later in the book, which showed how, in this context, significant differences were demonstrated.

9

Examples of the Use of the Grid Technique in the Clinical Situation

The value of any psychological testing technique rests upon its capacity to present the observer with accessible relevant data. The choice of technique will depend upon the nature of the subject's problem and the use to be made of the data by the observer. In a clinical setting, whether psychiatric or casework, the observer is usually engaged in an attempt to understand another's behaviour or symptoms in order to help him modify his behaviour towards a more satisfactory pattern and to lose his symptoms. Presuming that the patient or client's problems are not the result of organic impairment and not the effect of irreversible external constraints, this problem resolves itself into understanding the subject's world in terms of the definition of self and others, and the possibilities and choices which he sees as being available to him. An understanding of this allows the therapist or case-worker to predict the meaning to the patient of his own intervention, and hence makes it more likely that his intervention will be effective in giving help.

In the present chapter, a number of examples will be given where grid techniques have been used in clinical situations to answer questions relevant to the understanding, treatment and prognosis of patients or clients. Some of these histories are taken from the literature and some have not previously been reported.

The Arsonist: Why does a respectable and moral man commit arson, and is he likely to do so again? This example is taken from one of the earliest case reports in the British literature of the use of the repertory grid technique in a clinical setting, in a paper by Fransella & Adams (1965). This paper reported a single case example of a man of strict moral upbringing and beliefs who had committed a number of acts of arson. Grid techniques were used to investigate this case with a number of ingenious variations. In one of the tests applied, it was shown how the man in question saw himself as being like he would like to be in character, and this implied enjoying having power and believing that people got the punishment which they deserved. This characterisation was contrasted with the kind of person who might take pleasure in being sexually aroused and the kind of person who would commit arson. From this and the other tests carried out, the authors concluded that there was a real risk of further episodes of arson from this man, in view of the fact that, despite the history, there was such a high negative correlation (-0.9) between the sort of person he thought he was and the sort of person who might commit arson.

A Suicidal Act: Why does a girl make a suicide bid? A study of a suicidal act in a nineteen-year-old female student, Susan, was reported in my first paper on the grid technique (Ryle 1967). The following is condensed from this paper.

Susan consulted with depression due to the defection of her boy-friend, Brian. Brian, she said, was the most important thing in her life, but had latterly become ill-disposed and unkind and had formed a relationship with another girl. He said he wanted no more to do with Susan, although contact had been retained. Susan described Brian as weak, easily influenced, gullible, and having no idea of what he wanted beyond a wish to please everybody all the time. None the less, she felt she could not do without him. Her own family consisted of two parents and an older brother. She described her father as reliable and stable; though quiet, he 'was not really dominated by mother, although he might seem to be'. Mother, who worked as a business executive, was a driving person, always on the go. She was usually stable, but had been depressed recently due to the illness of Susan's brother; an illness which, from Susan's description, was probably an acute psychotic breakdown. Two weeks after consulting, Susan challenged Brian to a meeting to prove that he was not scared of her, or impotent. This meeting took place, but Brian was unwilling to continue the relationship, and Susan then took alcohol, fifty aspirin tablets and turned on the gas in her room— where she was found by friends while still conscious.

Both SUSAN and BRIAN completed a standard repertory grid shortly after the suicidal act, using some common constructs and elements. The aim of this grid was to answer two questions, namely: (a) what is the explanation of the attraction which binds

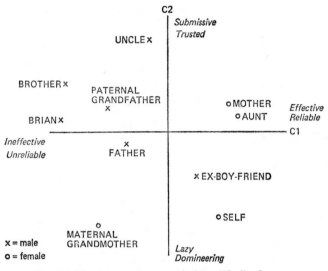

Fig. 9.1 Two-component graph (simplified) of SUSAN

SUSAN to BRIAN despite her uncomplimentary views of him, and which ties BRIAN to SUSAN despite his experience and fear of suffocation by her? (b) what made SUSAN attempt suicide? SUSAN's two-component graph is given in Fig. 9.1. In this grid and in Brian's grid (Fig. 9.2) a highly simplified version of the grid is provided, only key elements being included, the components being labelled by the constructs with the highest loading. It is seen that SUSAN construes herself as *domineering*, and that the MALE/FEMALE contrast in SUSAN's family constellation is between the more *effective* FEMALES and the *submissive* and *ineffective* MALES. SUSAN's position in relation to that of BRIAN represents, in exaggerated form, the balance which she perceives as characteristic for all relationships between the sexes.

BRIAN's two-component graph is given in Fig. 9.2. BRIAN's construction of the relative strength of SELF and SUSAN shows many similarities to the picture based upon SUSAN's grid, in that she has the highest and he one of the lowest loadings on the first component relating to strength. His position in relation to SUSAN is seen to repeat in an exaggerated form his position relative to his MOTHER.

The first two questions may now, to some degree, be answered. For SUSAN, relative ineffectiveness is an expected and appropriate

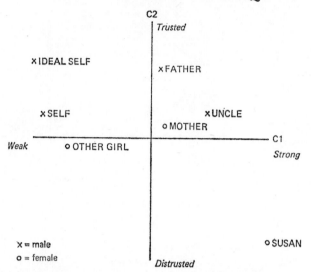

Fig. 9.2 Two-component graph (simplified) of BRIAN

masculine characteristic; whereas for BRIAN, relative strength is an expected female characteristic. Each finds in the other qualities which, though deviant in general cultural terms, are characteristic of their immediate families. For both BRIAN and SUSAN, this relationship is of more importance than other relationships with less disparate and more conventionally construed partners, e.g. SUSAN'S EX-BOY-FRIEND, BRIAN'S OTHER GIRL. However, BRIAN's distrust of SUSAN and resentment of her domination may be reinforced by the general cultural norm of masculine strength, and by the availability of trusted and strong male identification figures in his FATHER and UNCLE. In any case, he was able, however ambivalently, to challenge SUSAN's construct of him as *ineffective* and in doing so, he successfully challenged her construct of herself as *domineering*. One could argue that Susan's self-destructive act was carried out because to die seemed less painful than to face so radical a revision of her construct system; or that to threaten death represented a means of reassuring her power.

A third question, as to how far, following the reconciliation which took place after Susan's suicide attempt, there was a modification of the relationship, was investigated by re-testing four months after Susan's first test. In the interim, Susan had a brief period in psychotherapy, and the relationship with Brian was re-established. The changes between these two test occasions were modest; they affected Brian more than Susan and are described in full in the original paper, which concluded with the comment, 'One may anticipate that this change will set in motion a continuing modification of the construct systems, self-perceptions and perceptions of others of both subjects; but, if the relationship endures, it seems likely that Susan will continue to see Brian as relatively weak but affectionate; and Brian to see Susan as relatively strong but amiable.' As a postscript to this paper, it may be reported that Brian and Susan subsequently married, and three years and a child later, went through a very similar episode in which Brian's attempt to leave Susan was followed by a suicide bid on her part. This story provides, therefore, a good example of the repetition-compulsion (in analytical terms), or of the relative inertia of construct systems (in personal construct terms).

Two Drug-Users: Can this patient consider giving up drugs? Patient motivation is a very important factor in the success of any psychotherapy or casework intervention; and in the case of illegal drug use, where both the drugs and the sub-culture of drug-taking offer short-term gratification and some degree of personal validation, intervention will have very little chance of success unless there is a clear motive on the part of the patient. For this reason, it is important to concentrate the scant resources available for dealing with those involved in illegal drug use on those individuals who are realistically able to contemplate giving up the drug, and dealing with their underlying problems in a different way. That the grid may be of value here is shown by the following contrasting pair of multiple-self grids which were collected by R. R. Ryle and are reproduced with acknowledgment and thanks.

Case 1. The first case is that of a twenty-two-year-old girl living with her boy-friend, both using marihuana and LSD regularly and experimenting with other drugs from time to time, but not involved in regular opiate use. Elements in this grid included REAL SELF, SELF ON DRUGS, SELF AS BOY-FRIEND WOULD LIKE ME TO BE, SELF I FEAR I MIGHT BECOME, and the IDEAL SELF. The most salient construct in the grid was *moral*, which was positively correlated with *nervy* and *short-tempered*, negatively correlated with *imaginative*. The element THE SELF I FEAR I MIGHT BECOME accounted for 20 % of all the variance (there were nineteen elements in all). The two-component graph (Fig. 9.3) shows the REAL SELF identified with MOTHER as *emotional*,

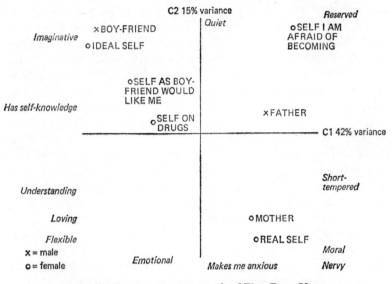

Fig. 9.3 Two-component graph of First Drug-User

nervy, moral and short-tempered. FATHER is seen as quiet and reserved and in the quadrant of THE SELF I FEAR I MIGHT BECOME; the latter element is very extremely loaded. The IDEAL SELF is close to the BOY-FRIEND and polar to the REAL SELF on both constructs, being seen as *loving, understanding, having self-knowledge, imaginative* and *logical*. This pattern suggests a splitting mechanism with the bad self identified with MOTHER and the good self with the BOY-FRIEND. When it is seen that the SELF AS THE BOY-FRIEND WOULD LIKE ME TO BE and the SELF ON DRUGS are both located close to the IDEAL SELF, we can understand that this girl will not easily consider abandoning drug use. While the underlying splitting mechanism is unresolved, drugs have the effect of reducing the dissonance between the SELF she sees as real and the SELF WHICH SHE WOULD LIKE TO BECOME, whereas drug use does not move her in the direction she fears.

Case 2. The second drug-user was a male with a history of school failure and of being in trouble with the police for violence. In this grid, also, the element the SELF I FEAR I MAY BECOME accounted for much variance (10% in a grid of nineteen elements). The large first component in the two-component graph (Fig. 9.4) contrasts *enjoys life* with *depressed, confused, violent* and *angry*. The elements with high loadings at the positive end are the IDEAL

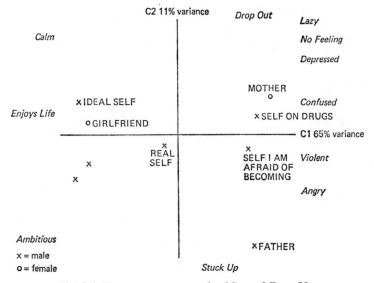

Fig. 9.4 Two-component graph of Second Drug-User

SELF, the GIRL-FRIEND and two MALE FRIENDS; while at the negative end are found the MOTHER, the SELF I AM AFRAID OF BECOMING and the SELF ON DRUGS. The REAL SELF is seen as located half-way between these two poles. In this case, there is obviously a negative valuation of the drug experience and therefore some hope that the treatment could be of value. The splitting along the first component between idealised and denigrated figures could, however, lead to difficulties if or when the idealised figures cannot sustain their ascribed idealised role. Both parents are relatively negatively placed, so that identification with either parent figure is no protection against drug use; indeed, the use of drugs leads to close identification with mother.

Persistent Depression: Why does this patient stay depressed? Rowe (1971b) reported the investigation of a woman, aged thirty-eight, who was depressed following hysterectomy. This patient completed a standard grid which was reported on as follows:

Mrs A.'s construct system has a simple structure which divides the people of her world into good and bad. The good people are *not critical of other people,* are *affectionate, easy-going, soft, generous.* They are *used by other people* but *do not complain.*

The bad people are *mean, hard, cruel, aggressive, nasty* and *hurtful, have no feelings,* are *fault-finding* and *self-opinionated* and *use other people.* This would be a workable system but for one thing; good people are *poorly*; bad people are *well . . .* Thus, if Mrs A. were to move from *poorly* to *not poorly,* she would also move from *soft* to *hard* and *cruel,* and from *generous* to *mean.* Is she were to move from *frightened* to *not frightened,* she would have to move from *shows affection* to *has no feelings,* and from *keeps worries to herself* to *can be nasty and hurtful.* The move from *like me* to *not like me* means leaving her daughter—with whom she identifies, and her husband and father—whom she values; and joining those people who reject her and whom she dislikes. To see herself as a good person, that is, to satisfy her conscience, she must be poorly. This is the construct system of the martyr, and such people resist having their suffering taken away from them.

The prediction was made, on the basis of this test, that the patient would show little improvement following treatment of her depression. In the event, Mrs A. had seven months' in-patient treatment, with three courses of E.C.T. and several changes of medication, without persistent improvement. Following discharge to out-patient care, and a further course of E.C.T., treatment was finally altered to one of social work intervention into the family—largely to give practical help with outstanding problems. Rowe concludes: 'It seems likely that many of the depressed patients who do not respond adequately to medication and E.C.T. construe their world in such a way that to be ill is a necessary outcome of the construct system.'

The Hypomanic Girl (Rowe 1971c): In this paper, a dyad grid was given to a twenty-three-year-old girl during a hypomanic episode, and was repeated one month later, after recovery. The Delta Index of General Consistency between the two testing occasions was 0.58, a low figure for so short an interval. The main changes were in respect of the correlations of constructs to do with *anger, fear* and *guilt,* and the programme also identified which elements were rated most differently on the two occasions, in particular showing the importance of the MOTHER. Rowe concludes her discussion of grid data in this case as follows:

The relationship of the MOTHER to SUSAN needs to be looked at separately . . . In the first grid, SUSAN showed her MOTHER as being somewhat *guilty about* and *frightened of* her; but in the second grid they share a perfect relationship ... However, when some statements are considered together, there emerges a picture of a mother who, at times, is cold and rejecting of her daughter. Perhaps more significant is the fact that on the first grid SUSAN stated that the person who frightened her most at the upper limit of the scale of *fear* was her MOTHER. It seems that, in a hypomanic state, SUSAN is fighting against a fear aroused by a perception of her world where she sees herself as *isolated*, *worthless* and *in danger*. In a calm state, she wants to see the world of relationships as warm and loving, but it seems that this perception is maintained by denial of some aspects of reality, especially in her relationship with her MOTHER.

Backward Readers: Why cannot boys of normal intelligence read? Leach (1971) carried out a study of retarded readers of normal intelligence, using a form of Ravenette's 'situations grid' (Ravenette, unpublished). With this form of test, the elements of the grid are simple line-drawings depicting situations relevant to the subject being researched—in this case, various reading and playing situations. In Leach's case, the drawings consisted of boys in various situations, some involving reading, and some not, and either alone, or in the company of mother, father and teacher. Ten retarded readers and ten controls (all boys) were investigated with this 'situations grid', and in addition, information was derived from teachers' reports and from interviews with the children and their parents. The constructs for the test were supplied. With this grid, Leach was able to show how, for each of the retarded-reading boys, reading carried with it some cost or negative implications, while this was not the case with the control boys. There was significantly greater variation in grid responses among the retarded boys than among the controls. The grid and interview data combined, in many cases, to show very clearly the origin of the reading difficulty, and to indicate the reason for the ineffectiveness of the attempts made to help. As an example, here is a condensed version of one of the individual studies.

Mark was aged 9 years, 3 months; his WISC IQ was 104 and his reading retardation 28 months. From his teacher's account, he behaved relatively normally in class, though showing some anxiety for adult attention. His achievement in arithmetic was average and his reading difficulty was, therefore, a specific learning problem. Interviewed alone, Mark appeared bluff and confident and took on the role of 'tough guy', although, at the same time, was anxious to please. He described his elder brother as being scared and helpless, 'can't do nothing', 'jealous of me', and 'I've got more money'. Mark's grid (Fig. 9.5) shows a major

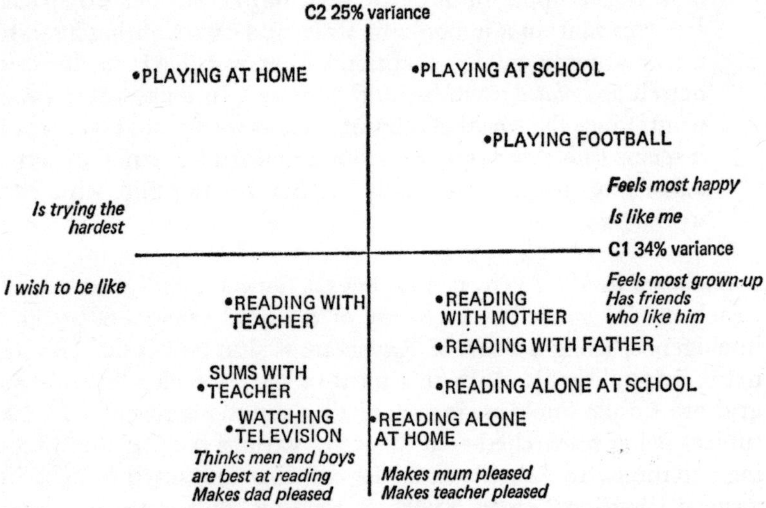

Fig. 9.5 Situations grid of a backward reader

split on the second component between the academic and non-academic situations, and a major split in the constructs. To be *happy* and *grown-up* is opposite to *pleasing adults*. The interview with this family threw some light on the origin of this situation. There was a marked contrast between Mark—seen as a villain—and his elder brother who was a good boy and a bookworm. Mark had to compete for affection with this good elder brother, and with younger siblings who occupied much of the mother's time. With neither goodness nor babyness on his side, he seemed to have opted out of the family and relied on his peer group. In this peer group, his 'tough guy', anti-academic stance was seen as crucial, and to become a reader implied losing this source of validation.

The Application of RG Techniques to the Study of the Process of Group and Conjoint Psychotherapy

The measurement of change after psychotherapy poses the same problem as the measurement of change after other forms of intervention, and grid methods can play a similar part. RG technique also offers, however, a means of assessing the process of group psychotherapy, in so far as the role of the self and other group members, including the therapist, can be recorded serially, by grid means, by each participant in the group. The constructs used in grid tests of this sort can be supplied, taking account of work already done in this field, notably the paper by McPherson & Walton (1970), who showed that experienced clinicians used three main dimensions in their descriptions of group members: *assertive* versus *passive*; *sensitive* versus *insensitive*; and *hindering* versus *helping* the group process. Alternatively, or additionally, the group itself can be invited to generate its own constructs. In a group of eight members, each testing occasion will generate eight versions of the current roles played by group members. Interpretation of this amount of data is demanding, for changes through time in the constructions placed on the self and others by each group member reflect both the effect of altered perceptions and of actual changes in behaviour. The consensus grid being developed by Slater can provide a picture, on each testing occasion, of the 'average' view held of the group, by the group; and the departure from this consensus of each individual member can be identified, but so far no work has been published using this method, and studies have concentrated upon selected variables only. Thus Smail (1972) used a grid technique to measure empathy between group members; and Watson (1972) listed some of the measures indicating psychodynamic factors likely to show change if group therapy were successful. Using a standard grid, completed by all group members on two occasions, Watson showed that the mean ratings of all elements on given constructs vary between occasions—suggesting that ratings were reflecting a group process—and also demonstrated differences in stability of construct means between patients and therapists. Variation around construct means also differed significantly between patients and therapists, and between occasions. The SELF/IDEAL SELF discrepancy, measured as a correlation between the constructs *like me* and *like I would like to be* was significantly different for patients and therapists. There were also differences in the stability of the first principal component. The likely psychological significance of these measures is discussed in the paper; and the need in future work to relate these changes to other indices of change is underlined.

I am currently engaged in developing a technique for recording change in couples undergoing conjoint therapy, which is analogous to this group work, but somewhat simpler. In this method, the couple complete a dyad grid in which their own relationship is rated 'when going well' and 'when going badly', and in which the relationships between the two parental pairs are also rated. This initial grid forms a backcloth, against which serial ratings of a couple's relationship, completed before each therapy session in respect of the preceding period, can be plotted. The elements in the serial grid, therefore, refer to SELF-to-OTHER and OTHER-to-SELF for the immediately preceding period, and change through time is indicated by the relative position of these elements. On completion of treatment, the initial form of grid can be repeated, to show whether the parental relationships have also been reconstrued in the course of therapy.

IO

Ten Psychotherapies

Psychotherapists commonly believe that they help some of their patients but this belief is challenged by many critics and is rarely backed by satisfactory evidence. In view of the cost of psychotherapy and in view of the uncertainty about which variables in the treatment situation affect outcome, the development of measures of change which can permit the comparison of different treatment methods, both as regards the nature and the degree of change achieved, is a matter of some importance. Such measures need to be both subtle and specific. A patient enters psychotherapy because of symptoms or because of a life problem, but the relationship between the presenting issue and the underlying difficulties is complex. The aims of treatment, and the decision as to what is possible in treatment, will vary between patients, therapists and situations. Attempts to devise simple criteria of cure, based upon an illness model of neurosis, are therefore unlikely to prove successful, and operational measures (e.g. of symptoms or of social adjustment), while of value, ignore the complexity of the problem. Symptoms and current difficulties are linked with the personality, internal object-relations and current personal involvements and social situation of the patient, and change can only be adequately assessed when these connections are taken into account.

It should be possible for psychotherapists to define their aims with a given patient and, as Malan (1963) has shown, it is both possible and, under most circumstances, necessary to work towards limited objectives. While therapists will wish to define these objectives in terms of their own theoretical background they can, to a useful degree, be re-stated in ways capable of testing, using repertory grid techniques.

One way in which this can be done was described in an account of a repertory grid study of a single patient (Ryle & Lunghi 1969). After initial clinical evaluation and repertory grid testing had been carried out the aims of treatment in this patient were defined in clinical terms and, on the basis of this, the direction of desirable changes in certain repertory grid measures and features, notably construct correlations and element distances, were recorded; subsequent re-testing with an identical test showed how far these changes had, in fact, occurred.

In the present chapter, the application of this approach to the study of ten patients is reported, these being the next ten patients seen, after the single patient already reported, who completed both the initial test and at least one re-test. This is essentially a descriptive account of the method used, not an experimental comparison of different treatment methods, and the only parallel rating of change was a crude clinical one. The patients differed widely and received a very different amount of treatment— assessment only in some cases, over 200 sessions in one. For each patient, certain construct correlations and element distance values were selected, on clinical and grid evidence, as being likely to change if treatment were effective, and this desired direction of change was recorded at the outset. Re-testing showed how far changes had occurred in the desired direction for each patient. To this extent, each patient can be considered as a separate experiment. In addition, however, it was possible to relate a number of changes to the study reported in Chapter 8, in which some grid features characteristic of neurotic subjects were identified. Changes occurring were classified according to whether the variables had shifted towards or away from the values characteristic of neurotics. The results in respect of those measures that were available are given in Table 10.1—not all the differences could be explored in this way, as the data on these patients were collected before the work reported in Chapter 8 was completed, and the grids had not been standardised in any way.

Case Histories

METHOD OF RECORDING

Each of the following ten case histories is presented in a systematic numbered order. Where the patient is included in the doctor's grid (see Ch. 12), the number is given so that the patient can be located on that grid. The headings are as follows:

1. Presenting complaint.
2. Psychopathological formulation.
3. Stage of treatment at time of last re-test, classified as not

treated, treatment ended by patient, treatment ended by agreement or treatment continuing. The total number of treatment sessions was recorded.

4. Test/re-test interval.
5. An overall clinical evaluation of improvement as nil, slight, moderate or definite, with a brief description of the change noted.
6. A description of the first repertory grid. The account given in these summaries notes salient constructs, names the constructs with the highest loadings on the first two principal components and describes the position of key elements in terms of these components.
7. Element distances: element distances indicate closeness or similarity between elements, values under 1 implying similarities greater than chance; values over 1, dissimilarity. Certain element distances were selected after the first test in respect of which it was predicted that change would occur if treatment were successful, the direction of change indicative of improvement being recorded. The initial value and the value on re-testing are recorded.
8. Construct correlations: in a similar way, certain construct correlations were selected which were thought liable to change in the event of the aims of treatment being achieved. The direction of such change as predicted initially and the first test and re-test values are recorded.
9. Other changes on re-test; for example, changes in the nature of principal components or marked element shifts are noted.
10. A concluding comment on the degree of change and on the relationship between the grid and clinical assessments of change is given.

Case Histories

The ten case histories are presented in random order. Details which might permit recognition of the subjects are altered or omitted. All the cases were personally assessed. Treatment, where given, consisted of weekly or twice weekly fifty-minute sessions in which interpretations were made along analytical lines. Two cases received group therapy from a colleague.

CASE 1: MALE ARTS STUDENT (Doctor grid patient 17)

1. Presenting complaint: depression and lack of confidence.

Table 10.1

Case Number:	1		2		3		4		5	
Test Occasions:	T1	T2	T1	T2	T1	T2	T1	T2	T1	T2
Element Distance: 1. SELF–IDEAL SELF	0.86	0.55*	1.30	1.24*	0.93	1.20	1.28	1.09*	1.15	0.633*
2. SELF–MOTHER	1.21	0.70*	1.15	0.91*	1.00	0.87*	1.09	0.92*	1.04	0.82*
3. SELF–FATHER	1.14	0.80*	1.32	0.82*	0.96	1.26	0.99	0.86*	1.15	0.74*
4. Number of elements at distance over 1 from SELF out of total number	15 — 22	4* — 22	20 — 24	6* — 24	15 — 26	19 — 26	9 — 15	5* — 15	17 — 27	4* — 27
5. Variation accounted for by first two components combined (percentage)	42	58	39	49	52	51*	58	61	46	54
6. Total variation about construct means	2035	2088	1951	1953	2308	1864*	778	818	2845	1213*
7. Percentage of variance accounted for by first component *times* loading of self on first component	119	37*	105	72*	52	219	205	141*	138	47
8. Ditto for second component	42	58	130	19*	19	333	61	60*	95	25
Number of positive changes (out of 8 possible)	5		6		3		6		7	
Clinical rating:	Slight		Mod.		Slight		Nil		Marked	

Table 10.1

6		7		8		9		10		No. Improved
T1	T3	T1	T2	T1	T2	T1	T3	T1	T2	
0.96	1.53	1.14	1.42	0.87	0.53*	0.45	1.06	0.9	1.25	5
1.39	1.06*	0.79	0.71*	0.97	1.10	0.87	1.02	0.95	0.95	7
1.25	0.96*	0.56	0.68	0.90	1.04	1.08	0.95*	0.63	0.92	6
$\frac{14}{17}$	$\frac{14}{17}$	$\frac{10}{18}$	$\frac{5*}{18}$	$\frac{3}{14}$	$\frac{6}{14}$	$\frac{3}{15}$	$\frac{5}{15}$	$\frac{5}{22}$	$\frac{12}{22}$	5
69	75	74	75	67	75	67	60*	66	64*	3
1383	1032*	1695	1331*	1371	1188*	1215	774*	2001	1719*	7
37	208	215	317	55	422	62	104	70	254	4
136	108*	134	13*	38	19*	86	76*	20	36	7
4		4		3		4		2		
Slight		Slight		Nil		Mod.		Slight		

2. Psychopathology: a depressed, isolated man whose sense of isolation, heightened by a working-class background, derived from his perception of his mother as strict, moody and unpredictable and (probably) from an unconscious wish not to overtake his admired but frustrated and under-achieving father.

3. Treatment category at time of re-test: treatment was ended by agreement after a total of some thirty group sessions.

4. Test–re-test interval: nineteen months.

5. Clinical evaluation of treatment: slight improvement. He gained in social confidence, became marginally more assertive and more realistic and less forlorn and depressed, but there was little evidence of resolution of underlying conflicts.

6. First grid:

Principal component: C1. Positive: *quiet, inhibited*
                                    Negative: *expressive, lively*
                            C2. Positive: *unstable, depends on others*
                                      Negative: *tolerant, determined*

FATHER had high loadings at the positive pole of C1 and negative pole of C2. MOTHER had a high loading on the negative ends of C1. SELF had a high positive loading on C1 and C2, i.e. as *quiet* and *unstable*. The IDEAL SELF was median on both components.

7. Element distances:

	T1	Desirable change	T2
Distance of SELF– IDEAL SELF	0.863	—	0.550

8. Construct correlations:

	T1	Desirable change	T2
Masculine—			
aggressive	−0.273	+	−0.297
ambitious	−0.125	+	−0.305
Kind—			
unstable	0.301	—	0.106
worries	0.346	—	0.190

9. Other features of re-test grid: MOTHER and FATHER are less contrasted and SELF is seen as more like MOTHER, and all three are less extremely loaded on the first two components on the re-test grid.

10. Conclusion: On grid evidence, masculinity remains passive and kindness, while less correlated with instability, is more incompatible with ambition. The clinical and grid evidence both suggest persistent problems.

CASE 2. FEMALE SCIENCE STUDENT

1. Presenting complaint: depression with phobic and somatic symptoms.

2. Psychopathology: uncertainty about femininity, difficulty with expressing aggression, probably based upon sibling rivalry and a bad relationship with a dominating grandparent.

3. Treatment category at time of re-test: ended by agreement after five sessions plus follow-up.

4. Test–re-test interval: eight months.

5. Clinical evaluation of treatment: moderate improvement. She became more assertive towards her boy-friend and coped better with the grandparent.

6. First grid:

Principal components: C1. Positive: *reliable, kind*
Negative: *ruthless, bullying*
C2. Positive: *domineering*
Negative: *submissive*

The SELF was rated at the negative end of C2.

7. Element distances:

	T1	Desirable change	T2
SELF–IDEAL SELF	1.300	—	1.242
SELF–MOTHER	1.147	—	0.911

8. Construct correlations:

	T1	Desirable change	T2
Like me—			
sensitive	0.133	+	0.679
able to achieve	−0.116	+	0.619
attractive to opposite sex	0.584	+	0.262
Jealous of—			
attractive	−0.569	—	0.152
good leader	−0.453	—	0.097

9. Other features of re-test grid: *Jealous of* and *trapped by* are no longer salient constructs. The construct *religious* shows a marked drop in the correlation with *I would obey*, from 0.562 to 0.045. The principal components have changed, C1 now contrasting *sarcastic* and *sulky* with *increases my self-confidence* and *I would like to resemble* and C2 contrasting *relies on authority* and *religious* with *a bully* and *domineering*.

10. Conclusion: The majority of changes suggest that there has been a growth in confidence as regards femininity and capacity. Her difficulty with aggression was probably associated with her religious beliefs; the change in the correlation of *religious* with *I would obey* shows that the implications of *religious* have altered. Grid evidence here suggests more change than was expected from the clinical rating.

CASE 3. MALE ARTS STUDENT

1. Presenting complaint: depression and loss of ambition associated with falling in love. There was an accompanying venereal disease phobia. He also complained of bursts of irrational anger at the sight of couples together in real life or on the cinema screen.

2. Psychopathology: there was a close tie with mother. Mother subsequently gave an account of a six-week hospitalisation at the age of two-and-a-half. It seemed likely that there were early separation problems and unconscious, unresolved oedipal rivalry, the depression representing internalised aggression and the loss of ambition representing a retreat from potency.

3. Treatment category at time of re-test: treatment was ended by the patient after six sessions; there was some follow-up.

4. Test–re-test interval: eight months.

5. Clinical evaluation of treatment: slight improvement. At follow-up contacts he reported lessening depression and fewer episodes of irrational anger.

6. First grid:

Salient constructs are *amoral, mean* and *accepts people as they are.*

Principal components:　C1. Positive: *generous, liked*
　　　　　　　　　　　　　Negative: *mean, disliked*
　　　　　　　　　　C2. Positive: *touchy, perfectionist*
　　　　　　　　　　　　　Negative: *amoral, attractive*

The second component polarises FATHER at the positive end from MOTHER and IDEAL SELF at the negative, SELF being intermediate.

7. Element distances:

	T1	Desirable change	T2
SELF–FATHER	0.961	—	1.262
IDEAL SELF–FATHER	1.162	—	1.296
SELF–IDEAL SELF	0.927	—	1.198

8. Construct correlations:

	T1	Desirable change	T2
Amoral— attractive to opposite sex	0.545	—	0.158
I feel close to	0.524	—	0.234
Mean—ambitious	0.606	—	0.461
Able to achieve— intolerant	0.515	—	0.080
domineering	0.518	—	0.585

9. Other features of re-test grid: salient constructs at re-test were *I could take my troubles to*, *affectionate* and *I like*. The evidence from the first grid of a connection between sexual attraction and amorality and of achievement with domination would fit in with the clinical hypothesis. Element distances and positions on the second component show some tendency to identify with MOTHER and re-testing shows some further cross-sex identification, but most of the construct correlation changes are in the desired direction, suggesting that some improvement had occurred.

CASE 4. MALE SCIENCE STUDENT

1. Presenting complaint: academic difficulty and depression.
2. Psychopathology: provisionally related to the loss of father at the age of puberty, producing depression and a pattern of passive resistance in relation to work due to unresolved oedipal problems.
3. Treatment category at time of re-test: not treated. Follow-up contacts showed a recurrence of academic difficulty with continuing unconscious passive resistance mechanisms, but some reduction in depression attributed to better social contacts.
4. Test–re-test interval: fifteen months.
5. Clinical evaluation of treatment: nil.

6. First grid:

The salient constructs were *sad* and *strong*.

Principal components: C1. Positive: *energetic, strong*
                             Negative: *weak, passive*
                        C2. Positive: *trivial, cold*
                             Negative: *sad, creative*

The SELF was seen as *passive, quiet* and *sad*; MOTHER and IDEAL SELF as *warm, friendly* and *strong*; MALE FRIENDS and FATHER (as remembered) were seen as *constructive* and *energetic*.

7. Element distances:

	T1	Desirable change	T2
SELF–FATHER	0.986	—	0.860
SELF–IDEAL SELF	1.282	—	1.09

8. Construct correlations:

	T1	Desirable change	T2
Academic success—			
strong	0.475	+	0.219
Warm—strong	0.086	+	0.222
weak	0.176	—	0.371
Cold—			
likely to succeed	0.408	—	0.398
Sad—creative	0.272	—	0.662

9. Other features of re-test grid: At re-testing the construct *sad* accounted for less variance (from 9% to 6%) and the construct *likely to need psychiatric help* accounted for more (from 6.7% to 10.6%). Element distributions show little change and the SELF is still construed as *sad, weak* and *passive.*

10. Conclusion: Some shifts in a favourable direction are indicated by changes in construct correlations but in general the grid evidence is in accord with the clinical formulation.

CASE 5. FEMALE ARTS STUDENT (Doctor grid patient 9)

1. Presenting complaint: confusion, depression and relationship difficulties.

2. Psychopathology: early deprivation (mitigated by a nurse) with subsequent idealisation of parents covering bitter antagonism, especially for mother. Marked splitting; feeling and achievement

were felt as incompatible and in relations with men she tended to take on a controlling role to impotent, damaged and, in some cases, drug-addicted males.

3. Treatment category at time of re-test: ended by agreement after thirty-six sessions.

4. Test–re-test interval: fifteen months.

5. Clinical evaluation of treatment: marked; there seemed to be a successful working through of ambivalence and resolution of the split between affection and strength. A probably permanent relationship with a boy-friend, who although gentle, was not compliant, had been established.

6. First grid:

Salient constructs were *ruthless*, *masculine* and *destructive*.
Principal components: C1. Positive: *warm, reliable*
                               Negative: *destructive*
                     C2. Positive: *admired, ruthless*
                               Negative: *makes me feel secure*

Seven FAMILY MEMBERS were at the positive pole of C2, whereas the SELF and two EX-BOY-FRIENDS were at the negative pole.

7. Element distances:

	T1	Desirable change	T2
SELF–MOTHER	1.040	—	0.824
SELF–IDEAL SELF	1.150	—	0.633

8. Construct correlations:

	T1	Desirable change	T2
Respected—			
ruthless	−0.090	—	−0.371
dominating	0.198	—	0.033
warm	0.516	+	0.559
happy	0.415	+	0.231
maternal	0.384	+	0.496
masculine	0.074	+	0.063
Self-confident—			
ruthless	0.405	—	0.230
warm	−0.254	+	0.139

	T1	Desirable change	T2
Masculine—			
ruthless	−0.154	−	0.142
respected	0.074	+	0.063
warm	−0.321	+	0.109
maternal	0.162	−	0.295

9. Other features of re-test grid: most of the changes in construct correlations suggest a considerable move towards the objectives of treatment. At re-testing the three most salient constructs were *makes me feel secure, hard* and *warm*.

10. Conclusion: clinical and grid evidence of improvement are largely in accord.

Case 6. Male Arts Student (Doctor grid patient 28)

1. Presenting complaint: acute nosophobia, history of long-term anxiety, social isolation.

2. Psychopathology: schizoid withdrawal, major oedipal problems with avoidance of potency in all situations other then intellectual. Splitting mechanisms, e.g. idealised girl-friend versus mother, incompatibility of affection and strength.

3. Treatment category at time of re-test: not completed (referred elsewhere on leaving area). Two-hundred-and-two sessions.

4. Test–re-test interval: first to second test, eight months; second to third test, four years.

5. Clinical evaluation of treatment: slight to moderate improvement. Treatment was initially centred upon the interpretation of marked withdrawal and paranoid defences. After some months in treatment there was a severely disturbed phase marked by regression and border-line psychotic manifestations. Thereafter, the main treatment themes were oedipal. The main defence mechanisms were splitting and projection. There was some working through in transference but in the interpersonal sphere he remained severely restricted.

6. First grid:

Salient constructs at first testing were *a good Christian* and *I would take my troubles to.*

Principal components: C1. Positive: *Good Christian, sensitive, potent*

Negative: *no real interests, submissive*

C2. Positive: *at ease*

Negative: *shy, lonely*

The SELF was at the extreme negative pole of C2. PARENTS were at the negative pole of C1. The idealised GIRL-FRIEND and admired TEACHERS were at the positive end of C1.

7. Element distances:

	T1	Desirable change	T2	T3
SELF–IDEAL SELF	0.962	—	0.891	1.532
SELF– EX-GIRL-FRIEND	1.108	—	0.949	1.589
SELF–FATHER	1.245	—	0.988	0.963
SELF–MOTHER	1.385	—	1.275	1.560
FATHER– HEADMASTER	1.385	—	1.275	1.560

8. Construct correlations:

	T1	Desirable change	T2	T3
Affectionate— potent	0.211	+	0.267	0.704
able to achieve	0.273	+	0.257	0.302
attractive to opposite sex	0.342	+	0.317	0.588

9. Other features of re-test grids: there was no major change in the principal components as regards construct or element loadings.

10. Conclusion: element distance changes between the first and third tests showed increased evidence of splitting mechanisms, while the construct correlation changes indicated some possible resolution. Thus, while the possibility of being both *affectionate* and *potent* is greater, the SELF is still seen as lacking in both respects, and as isolated from others. Grid evidence is a curb on therapeutic optimism.

CASE 7. FEMALE POSTGRADUATE

1. Presenting complaint: difficulty in relationships, particularly with men. History of severe eating problems and delayed puberty.

2. Psychopathology: splitting, men being seen as weak, castrated, or as powerful and exploitive. Rejection of femininity

FG—G

8. Construct correlations:

	T1	Desirable change	T2
Able to achieve —			
I like	0.450	+	0.209
superficial	−0.177	−	0.584
affectionate	0.068	+	0.600
conformist	−0.270	−	−0.747
Academic/Intellectual —			
understanding	0.008	+	0.244
able to achieve	0.252	+	0.694
I like	0.450	+	0.209
Strong character —			
affectionate	0.833	+	0.479
I like	0.761	+	0.491
understanding	0.279	+	0.533

9. Other features of re-test grid: there is some increased self-acceptance but the construct correlations show a diminished liking for those who are *strong*, *academic*, and *able to achieve*, which does not suggest any resolution of the academic difficulty. The decision to leave university was understandable in the light of these changes. (Follow-up: he returned after a year's intermission more clearly motivated and proceeded without further consultation or evidence of academic difficulty.)

10. Conclusion: the grid and clinical assessments are in agreement in showing that no fundamental change had occurred between the two testing sessions.

CASE 9. MALE ARTS STUDENT (Doctor grid patient 18)

1. Presenting complaint: somatic symptoms, notably gastro-intestinal, provoked by social situations.

2. Psychopathology: early deprivation and oedipal problems. Mother was seen as hostile and women were either dangerous or idealised. Father was seen as passive and the self was similar, exhibiting compliance and denial of, or retreat from, potency.

3. Treatment category at time of re-test: ended by agreement. Nine sessions over eighteen months.

4. Test–re-test interval: two months from first to second test; nine months from second to third test.

5. Clinical evaluation of treatment: moderate. Symptoms became mild and infrequent; he seemed less submissive but was still very dependent upon others' approval.

6. First grid:

Principal components: C1. Positive: *reliable, strong, I admire*
Negative: no constructs
C2. Positive: *academic, affectionate*
Negative: *aggressive, strong*

SELF is towards the negative end of both components, while FATHER is towards the positive end of both components. MOTHER and the GIRL-FRIEND are at the negative end of the first and the positive end of the second. The IDEAL SELF is near the SELF. There is a SCHOOL FRIEND with an extremely high positive loading on the first component. Those persons with whom contact was associated with physical symptoms all had high negative loadings on the second component.

7. Element distances:

	T1	Desirable Change	T2	T3
SELF–IDEAL SELF	0.452	+	0.701	1.661
MOTHER–GIRL-FRIEND	0.519	−	0.353	0.980
SELF–SCHOOL FRIEND	1.895	−	1.460	1.190

8. Construct correlations:

	T1	Desirable change	T2	T3
Strong personality— affectionate	0.234	+	−0.389	−0.149
Sociable—academic	−0.456	+	−0.402	−0.332

9. Other features of re-test grid: on re-testing (T3) C1 contrasted positive: *intelligent, creative, academic*, with negative: *takes things for granted, conventional*; and C2 positive: *self-centred, worrying*, with negative: *contented, stable*. The SELF was now positive on C1 and C2 and the IDEAL SELF was negative on C2 in common with the GIRL-FRIEND. Both PARENTS were negative on C1 and

awareness of his relationship difficulties, and by a slow and incomplete working through of these. This case suggests the need for a fuller understanding of the different sorts of grid change, in particular the distinction between element movement within the construct system and modification of the construct system deserves investigation.

The changes in these ten subjects in respect of eight grid measures are given in Table 10.1 (pages 82–3). These are the eight measures available which correspond to measures shown in the research reported in Chapter 8, to discriminate between the grids of neurotic and normal subjects. The values for the first and last tests are given in the table; where the change is in the direction of normal, the second value is marked with an asterisk. Variables 1–3 are based upon the tendency of neurotics to see themselves as unlike their parents and their ideal selves. Variable 4 reflects the neurotic's concept of the self as deviant. Variables 5 and 6 are two measures reflecting the tendency to polar judgments and variables 7 and 8 reflect a combination of this tendency with a concept of the self as extreme or deviant. All variables have higher values in neurotics than in normals.

It is apparent from the table that the eight variables recorded do not necessarily change in the same direction. The relation of each variable to clinical features is uncertain, and the weight to be given to any one measure can only be arbitrarily assigned. A simple summing of positive changes shows that the three patients rated clinically as marked or moderate improvement showed a mean of 5.6 positive changes compared to a mean of 3.9 for the remainder.

I I

Couples

Kelly's sociality corollary states that: 'To the extent that one person construes the construction processes of another, he may play a role in a social process involving the other person.' For most adults, marriage is the most intense and long-continuing social process experienced and one which would seem to offer the most opportunity to extend the accurate construction of the other; one also which one would expect to extract the highest price for failure to do so accurately. The relationship between marital adjustment and psychological stability in adults and in their children has attracted relatively little attention until recently; but there is now clear evidence that spouses resemble each other significantly in respect of neurosis (Pond *et al*. 1963; Kreitman 1962 and 1968) and there is strong suggestive evidence that this association represents the effects of interaction rather than of initial selection of like by like (Kreitman 1968; Kreitman *et al*. 1970). An association between similarity in respect of a number of attributes and characteristics and marital stability is well established (Tharp 1963), but this evidence does not include similarity in respect of personality where, indeed, in the view of some writers (e.g. Winch 1958) complementarity rather than similarity is the rule.

For an understanding of how the marital relationship and the emotional stability of the marriage partners may interrelate, we must turn to the clinical literature, notably that produced in the psychoanalytic tradition (e.g. Main 1966; Dicks 1967). Dicks identifies three levels of interaction in a marriage. The first level is the public one reflecting the social and cultural backgrounds and values of the couple. The second level reflects the more personal values and norms of the individuals, which may match or complement one another; disagreements at this level are coped with through the co-operation and effective problem-solving procedures of which mature, differentiated adults are capable.

positively for females with M.H.Q. scores ($r = 0.38$ not significant) and negatively for males ($r = -0.51$ significant at the 10%
level on the two-tailed T test). Should these sex differences prove
to be significantly present in a subsequent sample, this would be a
finding of some interest, suggesting that neurotic females are *more*,
and neurotic males *less* able to predict the other. The most interesting finding of the study was the demonstration of significant
differences between adjusted and maladjusted couples in respect
of the perceived resemblance between the SELF-to-PARTNER and
SELF-to-PARENT relationship, and the demonstration of the
differences between 'going well' and 'going badly' conditions of
the relationship. These resemblances were investigated through the
use of element distances, e.g. between the element SELF-to-
PARTNER and the element SELF-to-PARENT. It was found that
maladjusted individuals differed from controls in that they were
more likely to see the relationship of SELF-to-PARTNER as
resembling that of SELF-to-PARENT, and more likely to see the
relationship of PARTNER-to-SELF as resembling that of PARENT-
to-SELF. In maladjusted couples, the shift from the 'going well'
to 'going badly' condition, in respect of their own relationship
was accompanied by a perception of the self as becoming more
childlike (i.e. SELF-to-PARTNER moved closer to SELF-to-
PARENT), while the partner was seen as becoming less parent-
like—a situation likely to be experienced as doubly depriving.
These associations were more marked in respect of the parent of
the opposite sex. (These associations were demonstrated by two
forms of analysis, and were significant at p levels varying from
0.1 to 0.02.) These findings were from a small sample of young
couples and obviously need replication. As far as they go, however,
they seem consistent with the psychoanalytic view that patterns
of relating, based upon unresolved parental attachments, play
an important part in marital conflict.

Double Dyad Grid Before and After Conjoint Therapy: A Case Study

CLINICAL HISTORY

Barbara consulted a few months after she had begun to live with
Ernest. She had previously been seen at various crisis points in her
student career and had had one short period in individual psychotherapy. She had problems to do with work, in that she consistently under-achieved, and problems in her relationships with

men, which had been numerous, but marked by frigidity. Latterly she had become aware of some lesbian inclinations. With Ernest, she felt for the first time that she wanted an enduring relationship and hoped to overcome her previous pattern. The problem seemed to be one of splitting, with men being seen either as inoffensive and affectionate, or as exploitive and attractive. Ernest, although gentle, was not weak, but she remained entirely frigid sexually with him.

Barbara and Ernest were seen at a joint assessment and were offered conjoint therapy, which they accepted. The first double dyad grid was carried out at that time. From the early sessions, it seemed that Barbara's main fear was that of being engulfed, an anxiety stemming, it seemed, from her relationship with her parents who were seen as so good and so permissive that no angry feelings could be directly expressed within the family. With Ernest, her anger always took a passive form—withdrawal, sulking and frigidity. This behaviour seemed to feed into his main anxiety which was of being rejected. This fear led him to be placatory and, at times, childlike.

In the course of treatment, there was a growing freedom for both Barbara and Ernest to express negative feelings directly, and a growing capacity on Ernest's part to be assertive; this capacity developed only slowly, however, and, especially in the sexual relationship, Ernest continued to seem to need permission to approach Barbara and assumed that it would not be given; while Barbara could only feel that she wanted Ernest sexually when he was directly assertive. This problem was not entirely resolved when treatment was discontinued after a total of fourteen joint sessions spread over seven months. Grid re-tests were completed one year after the start of treatment, by which time the couple were married, and reporting continuing improvement.

REPERTORY GRID TESTING

(a) Saliency of constructs: for both BARBARA and ERNEST, the two most salient constructs were *sexually attracted to* and *dependent upon*. For BARBARA, the most salient element was the relationship of her MOTHER to her FATHER; while for ERNEST, the most salient element was the relationship of his MOTHER to HIMSELF.

Table 11.1   Construct correlations of BARBARA and
ERNEST on first and second testing occasions ;

	First occasion		Second occasion	
Construct correlation between :	BARBARA	ERNEST	BARBARA	ERNEST
Sexually attracted to with :				
submissive to	0.33	0.45	0.44	0.39
dependent on	0.49	0.63	0.91	0.56
understanding of	0.38	0.12	0.70	0.62
feels protective to	0.42	0.71	0.59	0.44
asks for sympathy from	0.41	0.70	0.77	0.32
affectionate to	−0.17	0.66	0.23	0.23
domineering to	0.43	−0.11	0.65	0.15
Affectionate to with :				
unwilling to communicate with	0.61	−0.56	−0.37	−0.14
feels protective to	0.11	0.86	0.49	0.81
asks for sympathy from	−0.18	0.79	0.43	0.16
feels rivalry for	0.24	−0.67	−0.28	0.15
Submissive to with :				
hostile to	0.68	−0.10	−0.33	−0.39
domineering to	0.61	−0.31	0.64	−0.62

listed, there is greater agreement than on the first occasion. The
most striking change in BARBARA's grid is in respect of the correlation of *affectionate to* with *unwilling to communicate with*, which has
gone from 0.61 to −0.37. For ERNEST the correlation of *affectionate to* and *feels rivalry for* has increased from −0.67 to +0.15,
and of *affectionate to* with *wants sympathy from* has decreased from
0.78 to 0.16. In the two-component graphs, Figs. 11.3 and 11.4,
it appears that both now see their own PARENTS' relationship
dyad as being parallel to their own, with the same relative sex-
roles. Both still see BARBARA as relatively *protective*.

OTHER PSYCHOMETRIC DATA

Both BARBARA and ERNEST completed the M.H.Q. on each
testing occasion. The scores are given in Table 11.2, from which
it is evident that BARBARA has relatively more, and ERNEST
relatively fewer neurotic symptoms at the end of treatment.

CONCLUSION

It is seen that the double dyad grid produced data which, on
the whole, were confirmatory of the clinical formulation, and

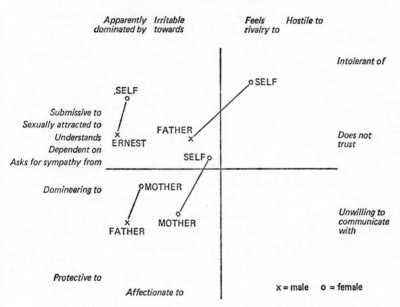

Fig. 11.3 BARBARA's second grid (selected dyads only)

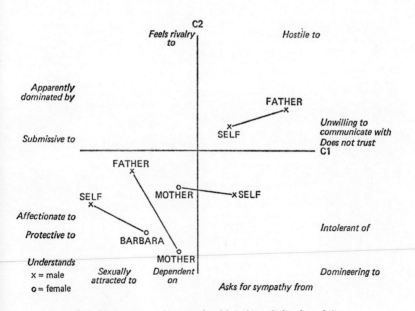

Fig. 11.4 ERNEST's second grid (selected dyads only)

Table 11.2 M.H.Q. scores on first and second test occasions for BARBARA and ERNEST

M.H.Q. scores		Anxiety	Phobic	Obsessional	Somatic	Depression	Hysteric
BARBARA	Test 1	4	2	4	1	2	4
	Test 2	6	5	10	1	3	5
ERNEST	Test 1	5	5	8	2	4	5
	Test 2	5	4	5	1	3	11

which, to some extent, supplemented it. Re-testing confirmed that changes had taken place in areas clearly relevant to the couple's original problem. This improvement, which both acknowledged and valued, was accompanied by an increase in symptoms for Barbara—a finding to bear in mind when assessing the outcome of psychotherapy by single or simple measures.

12

Repertory Grid Investigations of Professional Workers

This chapter illustrates some applications of repertory grid techniques to the study of doctors and social workers in their professional roles. My first venture in using grids in this way was an exercise in introspection. This is, perhaps, a less threatening process than submitting oneself to the enquiry of another, though in the event, the result, though revealing, was sufficiently interesting to make me publish it (Ryle 1969). The repertory grid test I carried out was designed to investigate my construction of patients. The elements were twenty-eight patients who were either in treatment with me, or had recently been assessed by me. The length of treatment varied from three or four sessions in some to over one hundred in others. The constructs included personality descriptions, reference to the history, and transference and counter-transference terms.

The two-component graph of this grid is given in Fig. 12.1. Elements are numbered in this graph, as a number of these patients are referred to elsewhere in the book. Constructs with low loadings on both components are omitted. In summary, the first component contrasts *makes me bored, makes me angry* and *passive–aggressive* on the right, from *I think can work with me* and *evokes sympathy* on the left. The second component distinguishes the *deeply disturbed* below, from the *expressive, amusing* above. The construct *has used drugs I think* has a high loading at the *expressive* end of this second component. It is worth noting that, at this time, the only illegal drug in common use was cannabis. Of those elements in the left half of the graph, only two out of thirteen are male, of those in the right half, ten out of fifteen are male. Part of this distribution may reflect an unconscious bias operating in case selection; but most of it is probably the result of the fact that more women students than men seek treatment on their own initiative, while more men than women are referred by tutors on

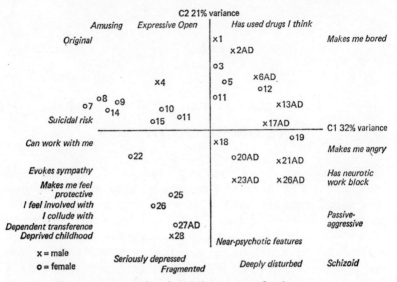

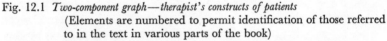

Fig. 12.1 *Two-component graph — therapist's constructs of patients*
(Elements are numbered to permit identification of those referred
to in the text in various parts of the book)
AD = in academic difficulty

account of academic difficulty. The right half of the graph contains a preponderance of students in academic difficulties (marked
AD). It is noteworthy that these students made me feel *bored* and
angry. One lesson I learnt from this experiment was to show greater
understanding of the tutor's frustration when faced with these
failing passive–aggressive students. That the teacher's 'counter-
transference' is, in fact, a good predictor of later academic difficulty was shown in a subsequent study in the Sussex University
Health Service, carried out by H. Clegg. In this study, the early
tutorial records of students who later failed were compared with
those of controls, and it was found that one highly significant
difference between the two was the frequency of tutorial comments
suggesting frustration, such as 'needs a kick', in the records of
students who subsequently failed.

Many of the observations made from this grid were news to
me, or at least were more clearly evident as a result of the test.
This was true particularly in respect of the evidence of the power
and nature of my counter-transference reactions to patients. Four
years later, it was possible to relate the patients' location on this
graph to the outcome of treatment. As regards the success, or

otherwise, of treatment, each patient was crudely rated clinically on a 4-point scale as showing definite (3), moderate (2), slight (1) or nil (0) improvement. Looking at each quadrant of the two-component graph in turn, the mean score of the eight patients in the upper left quadrant was 2.25, showing a good general level of improvement. That of the five students in the lower left quadrant was 1.4, while the mean score of those in the right upper quadrant was 0.55, and in the right lower quadrant 0.33. As regards the duration of treatment (defined as regular psychotherapy sessions at least once weekly), four of the five patients in the left lower quadrant received treatment for three or more years, whereas only one of all the remaining patients received treatment for as long as this.

These findings clearly had implications for my selection of cases for treatment, and for my own capacity to cope constructively with the passive-aggressive patient. More generally, the study served to throw open a way to study more systematically the operation of these factors in myself and my colleagues with the aim of relating some of the findings to more adequately rated measures of outcome. As a next step, with this aim, constructs were elicited from several colleagues and a shared list, based upon all these constructs, was evolved and applied by each doctor to his or her current case-load. Due to various problems, a full systematic study has not yet been completed, but an early and chastening experience was to find, from a study of the construct correlations in the grids of different doctors, that the consensus shared about the meanings of our mutually exchanged diagnostic terms was far from complete. A number of problems delayed a more systematic study in this area, notably staff changes, and some reluctance by therapists to carry out tests in this sensitive area, and the fact that knowledge about patients in long-term therapy is of a different order from knowledge about patients who have just been assessed. One by-product of these difficulties was the development of the sessional grid.

THE SESSIONAL GRID

The sessional grid takes, as the elements of the test, a patient session rather than a patient. The final grid is made up of the ratings of a number of sessions, either from one patient or from a number of patients. An example of such a grid, referring to a sequence of sessions in three patients in long-term therapy, is given in Fig. 12.2.* The constructs used in this grid were those developed from the preliminary studies referred to above, in which a number of construct pools from different doctors were combined, and only constructs deemed usable by all were retained. In practice, these constructs remained unsatisfactory to use in some ways. Fifteen of the constructs referred to sessional themes (i.e. to the main content of the session); nine referred to

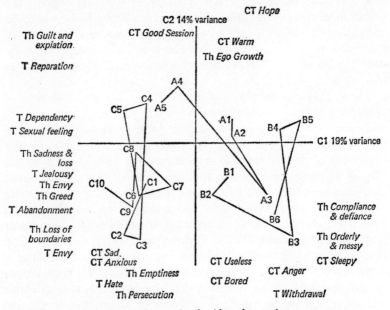

Fig. 12.2 *Two-component graph—sessional grid on three patients*
T = transference construct; CT = countertransference construct;
Th = themes of session

transference feelings acknowledged and/or interpreted during the session; and eight referred to counter-transference feelings experienced during the session, including, under this heading, one construct rating the overall value of the session. In the graph, constructs referring to transference are labelled T; and to counter-transference, CT. Constructs with low loading on both principal components are omitted. The patients were rated rapidly against the forty-one constructs on 7-point scales immediately after each psychotherapy session.

* It may be noted that the principal components account for an unusually small percentage of variance.

The clinical situation was as follows: All three patients were female students in their early twenties, and all were seriously disturbed. Cases A and B were in academic intermission because of their difficulties. Case A, in three times weekly therapy, had a severe schizoid disorder. Earlier in treatment, she had exhibited definite psychotic features. Case B, who was seen twice weekly, was a withdrawn, isolated girl with early problems relating to her mother, and later ones relating to difficulty in mourning the death of her long disabled father. Case C, also seen twice weekly, alternated between dependency and anger in the transference. Her history gave evidence of major separation problems, and at different times, she showed disturbance at oral, anal and genital levels. Case A was in her third year of treatment, and both B and C had been in treatment for approximately one year at the time of the test.

Inspecting the two-component graph, one can go clockwise from 12 o'clock, and look at the nature of the space defined by the construct loadings. From 12 o'clock, we pass from a positive counter-transference through an unlabelled segment to a region of negative transference and negative counter-transference in which themes of *compliance–defiance* and *obsessionality* occur. Continuing round the graph, the next zone (6 to 8 o'clock) represents severe paranoid schizoid disorder with themes of *persecution, emptiness* and *loss of boundaries.* Transference here is marked by *hate, envy, greed* and *feelings of abandonment,* and the counter-transference is one of *sadness* and *anxiety.* Further clockwise movement would seem to represent the shift into the depressive position, with feelings of *guilt, expiation, jealousy* and *exclusion.* The transference here is marked by *dependency, sexual feeling* and *reparation.* Counter-transference in this sector is marked by satisfaction with the value of the session. If one looks at the distribution of the three patients' sessions, it is evident that each is confined to more or less one area of the graph; but in all cases, major shifts occur from session to session. Case A is seen to alternate between the paranoid schizoid and depressive positions; cases B and C are alternately blocked and occupied with depressive and oedipal themes.

In terms of psychotherapy, six to ten sessions is a short time, and no conclusions could be drawn about the progress of these patients from this experiment; but it shows how this technique offers a means of illustrating the progress of therapy. The to and fro, or spiral tracks followed by these patients over the short term will be of no surprise to therapists. Clearly, the range of constructs used is probably, and the counter-transference pattern is inevitably, an idiosyncratic one. The experiment can in no way claim to test or validate the theory upon which therapy was based; but it is, perhaps, of some comfort to see a degree of internal consistency in the application of the theory to these cases, and the explicit location of counter-transference constructs in relation to the constructs recording patient variables is of interest and of potential value. The method, in fact, would seem to offer a useful means of examining and making more explicit the therapist's involvement in therapy, and may, therefore, contribute to psychotherapy research.

MEASURES OF THERAPIST EMPATHY

A further use of the repertory grid technique to investigate the therapist's involvement in treatment is to use it to investigate the therapist's capacity for accurate empathy. The Delta program (see Chapter 5) can be used to compare a patient's grid with the grid predicted for him by his therapist, and the degree of the therapist's empathy and the localisation of his misunderstanding can be identified. The first papers describing this technique were by Watson (1970) and Rowe (1971a). Rowe used a standard grid with some elicited and some supplied constructs. Twenty people known to the patient formed the elements of the grid; these were dichotomised on each construct by the patient, and by the psychiatrist treating the patient, as he predicted the patient would do it. The overall Index of Consistency between the two grids was 0.32; and the Delta grid of change showed that the major mismatch occurred in relation to one particular construct, and to one element. In a similar study, using the dyad grid (Ryle and Lunghi 1971), with a patient who had been in psychotherapy for over two years (patient No. 7 in Fig. 12.1), the Index of General Consistency between the patient's and the therapist's predicted grid was 0.50. Ranking the twenty-four dyad elements in order of accurate prediction, the five most accurately predicted were the elements SELF-to-FATHER, THERAPIST-to-SELF, MOTHER-to-SELF, FATHER-to-SELF and SELF-to-THERAPIST—that is to say, those most immediately accessible to the therapist and most discussed in the course of therapy. Examination of the inter-grid matching for the constructs showed that the worst predictions were for *frustration*, *anger*, *threat*, *control* and *guilt*, and demonstrated in particular the failure of the therapist (myself) to construe the patient's view of him as being threatening; perhaps the position of this patient in my construct space (see Fig. 12.1) may have contributed to this underestimation of negative feeling.

Accurate empathy is held to be a key variable affecting the outcome of therapy (e.g. Truax *et al.* 1966). The use of the grid in the way described here seems to offer a means both of measuring this variable and, possibly, of enlarging the therapist's capacity for it.

PERSONAL FACTORS AND CHANGE IN SOCIAL WORK TRAINING

Arising out of the work with doctors' grids, a study of social work students in training was undertaken. Students participated in this voluntarily and the results of the testing were available only to them and the researchers although, in some cases, the students did discuss the results with their tutors. In the first group study, a standard grid was used incorporating four supplied constructs (*makes me feel anxious, makes me feel angry, makes me feel competent,* and *I am indifferent to*) and twelve elicited ones. The sixteen elements included SELF, IDEAL SELF AS PERSON, IDEAL SELF AS SOCIAL WORKER, TUTOR, SUPERVISOR and some CLIENTS. The aim of the study was to see how far potential problems in the social work role could be identified from grid interpretations, and to investigate, through re-testing, how much change occurred during training, the test/re-test interval being somewhat over a year. An example of such a grid, modified in detail, done by a male social work student, is given in Fig. 12.3. *Secure in self* correlated at −0.54 with *makes me anxious* (i.e. insecure people may make him anxious), and *makes me angry* correlated at −0.7 with *expressive* (i.e. people who cannot express feelings may tend to make him angry). On the two-component graph, SELF, IDEAL SELF, TUTOR, SUPERVISOR and FRIENDS cluster at the *flexible, expressive* end of the large first component. This group is separated from four CLIENTS at the other end of this component (who *make him angry* and *anxious*) and from two with high loadings at the *introspective* end of the second component. The conclusion drawn from this, which was discussed with the student, read as follows:

> Insecure people who cannot express feelings arouse anger, anxiety and a sense of incompetence. The high percentage of

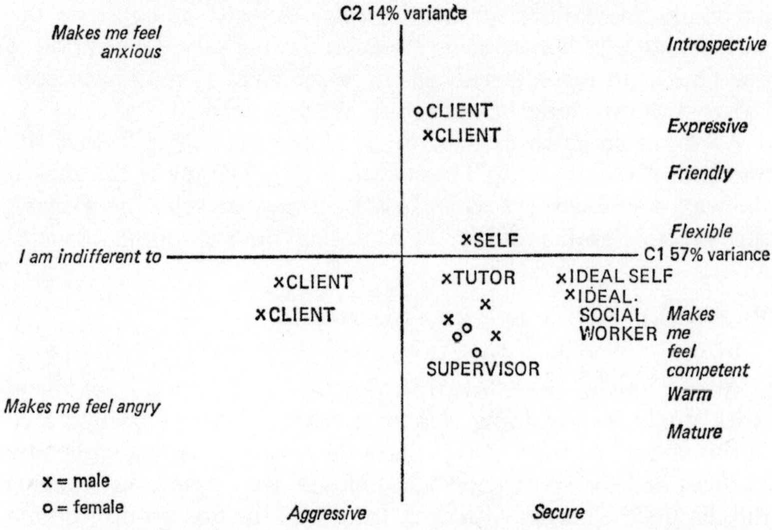

Fig. 12.3 *Two-component graph—social work student (initial test)*

variance accounted for by the first component, and the distribution of elements suggests a defensive identification with the normal, and the small SELF/IDEAL SELF separation suggests a low motivation to change. It could be that there is a denial of anxiety and bad feelings in the SELF which would need to be worked through to enable effective casework to be done.

Re-testing this student near the end of training showed considerable changes. In respect of the construct correlations, changes had occurred in the direction predicted as desirable, as is shown in Table 12.1. The second two-component graph (Fig. 12.4) shows

Table 12.1   Construct correlations before and after social work training

Correlation	First test	Desired shift	Second test
Secure with *makes me anxious*	0.54	Negative	−0.32
Secure with *makes me feel competent*	−0.34	Positive	0.39
Makes me angry with *able to express feelings*	−0.70	Positive	−0.14

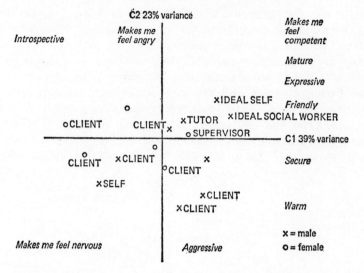

Fig. 12.4 *Two-component graph—social work student (re-test)*

diminution in the size of the first component, i.e. a less one-dimensional view of the world, and a much less extreme polarisation between CLIENTS and 'NORMALS'. There is now a poor self-concept polar to the ideals. This second test was reported as follows:

> The change here suggests that the defences which were postulated in the report on the first testing occasion were penetrated in the course of the training. This has resulted in desirable shifts in the construct correlations in that he no longer is liable to feel *anxious* and *incompetent* when faced with *secure* people, and is no longer liable to be *made angry* by people who *cannot express their feelings*. There is, however, a poor self-concept. It is to be hoped that further experience of his own professional competence may lead to a greater degree of self-acceptance.

In later work with social work students, the dyad form of grid was used to investigate the relationship between the perceived reciprocal roles of the student with parents, with tutors at the University, with field supervisors and with clients. Construct correlations were used to investigate the implications of the social work role as in the above example. An unexpected finding of this study was the large number of students in whom the SELF-to-CLIENT dyad was parallel to the SELF-to-PARENT dyad. To have played a supportive role to parents (or to one parent, for in many cases only one parent survived) was evidently a common antecedent to the choice of social work as a career. The importance of the TUTOR-to-SELF and SUPERVISOR-to-SELF relationship as a role model for the SELF-to-CLIENT relationship was also demonstrated. Over the two years' training, the majority of students showed greater role confidence and their construct systems became more complex. This study will be reported in full elsewhere

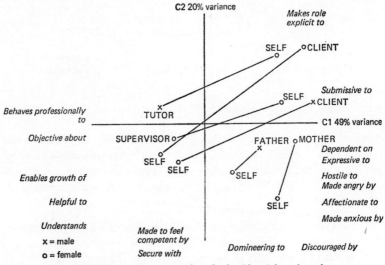

Fig. 12.5 *Two-component graph—dyad grid social work student*

(Ryle & Breen, in press). To close this chapter, an example of a dyad grid of a social work student from this series will be given.

In this group study, all the constructs were supplied and the role-titles and number of elements was constant (except in the case of students with only one parent). As a result, construct correlations could be compared across grids, and the value for the given correlation in an individual student could be expressed as high, median or low, by reference to the distribution of values for this sample. The two-component graph of a student from this sample is given in Fig. 12.5. The construct *behaves professionally towards* correlated at very low levels with the constructs *makes role explicit to, hostile towards, submissive towards, dependent upon,* and

values the relationship with. The construct *feels affectionate to* correlated with *angry with* at 0.45. Looking at the two-component
graph, one can summarise the nature of the space as follows: the
right lower quadrant shows intense ambivalent feeling and the
left lower quadrant shows professional helpfulness. The left
upper quadrant is unlabelled, but by implication implies non-
involvement, and the right upper quadrant includes *submissive to*
and *makes role explicit to.* The report on this grid concluded as
follows:

> It is likely that problems will arise here from the ambivalent
> cluster of feeling which is highlighted by the strong positive
> correlation between *affectionate* and *angry*. From the two-
> component graph it appears that the relationship with the
> parents probably underlies this ambivalence. There is a
> possibility that professional relationships are sought as a
> means of creating manageable involvement, where powerful
> and confusing feeling can be avoided. Insofar, however, as
> clients are likely to evoke ambivalent feelings in the course of
> the case-work relationship, this professional detachment can
> only be coupled with effective social work functioning if
> the ambivalence of the self is recognised and come to terms
> with.

13

Construct Organisation
Some Theoretical and Practical
Considerations

Kelly's organisation corollary represents his main theoretical statement about construct interrelationships; but it is an aspect of his theory which has provoked little in the way of experimental validation, and which has been largely ignored in the use made of the repertory grid technique. This, I believe, is due in part to ambiguities in the way in which Kelly formulated this part of the theory, and in part to the fact that other modes of examining construct interaction have proved of practical value in the analysis of repertory grids, so that the hierarchical model has seemed largely redundant. The only direct attempt to investigate this area was the work of Hinkle, with the 'implications grid' (Bannister & Mair 1968). This is not a normal repertory grid, for no elements are used. Subjects provide, or are presented with a range of constructs and each construct is paired with each other construct, and the subject states which of the two implies the other. As a further step, the subject is asked to state at which pole of each bi-polar construct he would like to be placed. He is then asked to discuss the implications of being changed to the other pole of this construct. For example, a subject at the *wise* end of the construct *wise–foolish* would be asked to give the reasons for his preference for being at the wise end. He might, for example, say that to be *foolish* is to be *disregarded*, whereas to be *wise* is to be *admired*, and this is taken to generate a more superordinate construct, namely *admired* versus *disregarded*. This procedure is repeated with the higher order constructs (the laddering technique) in order to identify constructs of greater and greater generality and wider and wider implications. This procedure ensures that the subject generates a construct hierarchy, but the test procedure is far more divorced from everyday construing than is the case with a construct–element grid, and tends to generate findings which are either obvious or of uncertain significance; no work of clinical interest seems to have emerged from this approach so far.

A Clarification of Kelly's Organisation Corollary

Kelly's organisation corollary states that 'Each person characteristically evolves for his convenience in anticipating events, a construction system embracing ordinal relationships between constructs' (Kelly 1955). While Kelly elaborated a great deal of plausible sense from this proposition, he also generated (uncharacteristically) some confusion around it, which may explain why empirical investigations of construct organisation remain few. In the first discussion of the organisation corollary (p. 57) Kelly defines a superordinate construct as one which may subsume another construct as an element, but he at once offers two interpretations of 'subsume'. On the one hand, a superordinate construct can 'extend the cleavage line' of a subordinate construct, thus *good versus bad* can include, along with much else, the distinction implied by *clever versus stupid*. On the other hand, Kelly states that a superordinate construct may 'abstract across' the subordinate one; for example, the subordinate construct *clever versus stupid* may be placed on the continuum defined by the superordinate construct *evaluative versus descriptive*.

Kelly's dual use of the concept of superordination recurs through the book; for example, the following passage (p. 136) would seem to imply a 'more general' version of superordinacy: '. . . constructs may be used as viewpoints for seeing other constructs as in the hierarchical relationships of constructs within a system. In that sense, superordinate constructs are versions of those constructs which are subordinate to them.' On p. 479, however, a 'construct construing' definition is firmly propounded: 'A construct is construed as superordinate to another if the other is utilised as one of its contextual elements.'

Kelly's confusion is echoed by Bannister & Mair (1968). In their references to superordinacy, they usually describe the 'more general' type, but when confronted by the ambiguities implicit in Kelly, they offer a resolution which seems to serve only to add to the confusion. This, simply, is to state that elements are constructs, specifically (p. 126): '. . . constructs within the range of convenience of a superordinate structure . . .'—an assertion which raises the question of what status to accord to the distinction (or construct) 'construct versus element'. Slater (1969), in a more extensive discussion of this confusion, rephrases this distinction as 'operator versus operand' and is rightly emphatic about the essential importance of retaining it.

The two forms of superordinacy referred to above as the 'more general' and the 'construct construing' are essentially very different. The 'more general' form is exemplified by taxonomic classifications and superordinate–subordinate construct relationships of this type can be elicited by Hinkle's laddering technique (Bannister & Mair 1968). This type of superordinate construct is applied to the same elements as its subordinates. The construct construing type of superordinate construct, while seldom made explicit, is in use continually, in the choice of appropriate constructs; 'appropriate' in this sense means both 'for the task' and 'for the element pool to be construed'. Inappropriate superordinate construing of this type is the basis of some forms of humour and thought disorder. A superordinate construct of this type is *not* applied to the elements which are construed by its subordinates. Failure to distinguish these two forms of superordinacy can only lead to confusion.

In the construction of grids, the experimenter, to a considerable degree, predetermines—either explicitly or implicitly—the range of constructs used by the subject, and little or no attention is usually paid to the process whereby the subject decides which constructs to use. For certain purposes, this process, which represents the activity of 'construct construing superordinate constructs', might prove to be related to psychological processes of a more fundamental interest than those accessible to ordinary grid technique. This area seems potentially researchable, but so far neglected, perhaps in part due to the confusion surrounding the organisation corollary.

Alternative Ways of Displaying Construct Relationships

The work reported so far in this book has been based largely upon the analyses of grids with the Principal Component Programme of Slater, in which both mathematical expressions of interrelations, and their graphic display, have been examined. An alternative mode of display has been elaborated by Makhlouf–Norris *et al.* (1970, 1973), who investigated construct and element interaction separately. These authors define superordinacy in constructs as representing a high degree of intercorrelation with other constructs, a definition not following logically from Kelly's corollary, but obviously representing an interesting attribute of the construct. The main contribution made by these authors was their way of displaying graphically construct relationships. A level of construct intercorrelation was chosen as a cut-off point (the level being that which would indicate significance at the 5 % level, if significance were an appropriate concept in this context). Using this cut-off point, they showed that constructs could be located: (a) in primary clusters within which all constructs inter-related significantly; (b) as linkage constructs in which the construct correlated significantly with some of the constructs in more than one primary cluster; (c) as isolates correlating significantly with no other construct; (d) as secondary constructs correlating significantly with some, but not all, the constructs in the primary cluster. In their first paper, they showed differences between the structure of obsessionals and controls. Obsessionals tended to have monolithic structures in which most constructs interrelated in a single primary cluster, with perhaps a few isolates; or, in one case, a segmental structure in which there were two such clusters with no linking constructs. Controls, on the other hand, tended to have articulated structures with two or more distinct foci linked by constructs with significant correlations with both clusters. Clearly, in the monolithic structure, change in any one construct carries implications for all the others, and this feature is linked in their work to the rigidity of obsessional thinking. Further investigation, along these lines, is under way. It appears that depression is also associated with monolithic structures. These authors also describe a means of plotting element distances in which they focus upon the relation of self and ideal self to other elements.

The Location of Change in Construct Systems

It is often important to know whether, and in what ways, a person can change—particularly in selecting patients for different treatment procedures. The repertory grid technique may offer a means of doing this. As a preliminary move towards recognising, from grid data, the possibilities of change, a study was carried out (with Dana Breen) to test two hypotheses: (1) that constructs accounting for a high percentage of total variance in a grid would prove more resistant to change; (2) that constructs with a large number of strong intercorrelations with other constructs would prove more resistant to change.

Five groups of subjects were studied—all of whom had completed re-tests with identical repertory grids, after an interval of between one year and twenty months. Nineteen psychiatric patients and twelve social work students completed dyad grids on two occasions, and eight patients, seven students in academic difficulty without major neurotic problems, and nineteen controls completed standard grids on two occasions. The two grids of each subject were compared, using the Delta program, and the three least and three most stable constructs were identified. The attributes of these two groups of constructs in the first repertory grid were now compared, in respect of the percentage of variance accounted for, and in respect of the number of significant intercorrelations. The number of cases in which the predicted difference occurred is recorded in Table 13.1. It is seen that predicted differences occurred to a significant degree in respect of the percentage variance in both the dyad and standard grids. Differences

Table 13.1 Differences between constructs showing high and low stability between test and retest. The 3 most and 3 least stable were compared in terms (a) of % variance accounted for and (b) of number of significant correlations with other constructs in first test. (* $p < 0.05$. ** $p < 0.01$)

Sample	No.	Type and size of grid (Elements × Constructs)	Number with predicted difference in respect of % variance	Number of significant intercorrelations
Social workers	12	Dyad 16 × 20	12	12
Patients	19	Dyad 24 × 16	17	11
ALL DYADS	31		29**	24*
Patients	8	Standard 16 × 16	6	5
Students in academic difficulty	7	Standard 16 × 16	5	5
Controls	19	Standard 16 × 16	14	5
ALL STANDARD GRIDS	34		25*	15 N.S.

in respect of the number of significant intercorrelations occurred significantly in the predicted direction in the dyad grid, but not in the standard grids—in the latter, the control group showed a reverse tendency.

This work needs replication, but potentially might prove of interest and value in predicting the outcome of treatment or other change experience. In this same study, constructs showing high and low stability were sorted blind between those referring to strong versus weak affects, or to affects versus descriptions. On these distinctions, there was no significant difference in stability; so it seems that the face content of a construct—in this respect at least—was less related to its stability than were the selected characteristics derived from the grid.

Construct Interaction Investigated by Splitting Grids

The mean value for the association between any two constructs is derived from their varying associations as they are applied to all the different elements. This mean value may conceal not just random, but systematic variation between construct relationships. For example, in a given grid, *strong* and *dangerous* could correlate at +0.7, but this value could be the result of a correlation of +0.95 for the bulk of the elements and of −0.8 for the small subgroup. If this sub-group can be distinguished from the other elements by one of the subject's own constructs (for example, *friendly*), then one is demonstrating construct interaction, in that the correlation between *strong* and *dangerous* is a function of the element's position on the construct *friendly*. In the general proposition 'the rating of elements on construct A influences the implication of their rating on construct B for their ratings on construct C', A, B and C might, or might not, be interchangeable. As this seemed to be a proposition of theoretical, and possibly practical, interest, the following empirical study was carried out.

Seven grids were dichotomised, elements being divided into two equal-sized groups: (a) at random; (b) according to their ratings on some of the subject's more salient constructs; (c) (in one case) by the sex of the elements. All these grids were derived from student patients or controls and were standardised to the extent of having sixteen elements and sixteen constructs of which eight were supplied. The resulting pairs of half-grids, with eight elements each, were compared on the Coin program (Slater 1972). This programme gives a measure of overall similarity and also allows comparison, between the two grids, of the values of each construct correlation. Construct correlations differing between the two half-grids by an angular distance of 60° or more were listed.

The results are summarised in Table 13.2. This shows wide variations in the degree of difference between the two half-grids. In many cases, the random split has produced relatively low values for consistency due, doubtless, to the small number of elements, and the values are lower than those obtained from splitting on the bases of construct ratings in some instances. Meaningful construct interaction cannot be deduced from these cases.

Marked differences were found in three subjects only, namely (see Table 13.2), in cases 1. and 3. in respect of one construct only, and in case 7. which has been selected for further study because it shows the most considerable differences.

This is the grid of a student who had presented with depression, passivity, and academic failure. His grid was analysed on the standard Ingrid program of the M.R.C. unit for processing repertory grids. The principal component analysis of the grid showed a large first component accounting for 65.6 % of variance. The elements of this original grid were dichotomised five times to form two grids of eight elements each. The elements were split, (a) at random; (b) by sex; (c) according to their ratings on three constructs, two of which had the highest positive loadings on the first principal component, and the other of which had the highest negative loading. These dividing constructs were: *a worrier*, *approachable*, and *callous*. The two half-grids resulting from each of these splits were compared, using the Coin programme which gives (a) an overall measure of similarity, the coefficient of convergence with a value between −1 and +1 and (b) tables of construct correlations (also expressed as angular distances) for each half of the grid. It will be seen from the table that a large number of construct relationships differed by more than the 60° level in the two half-grids produced by the splits. Looking at the splits based on the dividing constructs, it was found that, in each case, among the construct correlations differing by over 60° was the correlation between the other two dividing constructs. Thus, in the more *callous* elements, the construct correlation between *approachable* and *worried* was −0.143; whereas in the less *callous* elements it was +0.936. In the more *worried* elements, *callous* and

Table 13.2 Grids split at random and by element ratings on selected constructs: coefficient of convergence between the resulting half-grids and the number of construct correlations differing by an angular distance of 60° or more between the two half-grids

Case No.	Basis of element split		Coefficient of convergence (Coin)	Number of construct correlations differing by angular distances of 60° or more
1.	Construct:	*Likely to need psychiatric help*	0.130	20
	,,	*Passive*	0.753	6
	,,	*Likely to succeed academically*	0.366	16
	Random		0.648	12
2.	Construct:	*Likely to succeed academically*	0.522	3
	,,	*Likely to need psychiatric help*	0.414	6
	,,	*Active*	0.153	11
	Random		0.153	13
3.	Construct:	*Strong character*	0.437	9
	,,	*Passive*	0.431	9
	,,	*Someone you can talk to*	0.129	22
	Random		0.476	6
4.	Construct:	*Active*	0.453	5
	,,	*Calm in crisis*	0.478	5
	Random		0.352	9
5.	Construct:	*Passive*	0.446	5
	,,	*Warm*	0.315	10
	,,	*Arrogant*	0.400	4
	Random		0.474	7
6.	Construct:	*Warm*	0.295	12
	,,	*Quiet in conversation*	0.361	11
	Random		0.456	5
7.	Elements:	MALE/FEMALE	0.552	6
	Construct:	*Worried*	0.254	12
	,,	*Approachable*	0.359	19
	,,	*Callous*	−0.677	27
	Random		0.744	3

approachable were correlated at 0.143; whereas in the less *worried* elements this correlation was −0.898. Finally, in the more *approachable* people, *callous* and *worried* correlated at 0.043; whereas in the less *approachable* people they correlated at −0.778.

These interrelationships make psychological sense which may be summarised as follows: it is safe to approach *worried* people who are not *callous*, and not safe to approach *callous* people who are not *worried*. If people are not *approachable* then *callousness* and *worry* are assumed not to go together.

Further information about the subject was obtained from examining the differences in construct correlations for male and female elements. It appeared that, for this subject, *active* women appeared as *strong*, *ambitious* and *callous*; whereas *active* men tended to be *not strong*, *unambitious* and *not callous*. In this case, the construct male–female was not explicitly present in the test, but can be seen to have acted as a construct with construct–relation modifying properties.

The theoretical implications of this case are that it provides evidence of non-hierarchical construct interactions and, in terms of the general proposition on construct interaction given above, A, B and C were shown to be interchangeable. The interchangeability of A, B and C is not, however, universal. In the other grids studied, whereas A influenced the correlation of B and C, construct B did not influence the correlation of A and C in most cases—at least not at the level of 60° angular distance chosen for this study. On the basis of the seven cases described, it seems that construct interaction of the form investigated may, or may not, be demonstrable. The interaction, when it occurs, is not necessarily hierarchical, but some constructs may influence others more than they are influenced by others. The conclusion that constructs interrelate in this way is not, on reflection, particularly startling, but this form of interrelationship appears to have been neglected in formal personal construct theory up to now.

There are some practical implications from this demonstration of construct interaction. The expression of the construct relationships in a grid through intercorrelations and the principal component analysis represents a valuable simplification, enabling the observer to look at the wood rather than the trees. For most clinical purposes this kind of analysis is adequate and the additional information derived from element splitting would not justify the labour. There may, however, be issues which can be clarified by this approach. For example, assumptions about sex-roles may become apparent when male and female elements are separately analysed, as in the case above. Another area where splitting may yield data of importance is in the dyad grid where separate analysis of self-to-other and other-to-self elements may produce psychologically interesting information.

It will be recalled that, in this form of grid, each dyadic pair generates two elements, and where the self is included in all the pairs, one can split the grid into self-to-other and other-to-self

Table 13.3 Construct pairs differing by more than 60° in angular distance as between SELF-to-OTHER and OTHER-to-SELF element grids

	Grid of SELF-to-OTHER elements		Grid of OTHER-to-SELF elements	
Submissive towards—dependent on	−0.345	110.2	0.759	40.6
Submissive towards— feels inadequate beside	−0.382	112.5	0.808	36.1
Domineering towards— protective towards	0.912	24.2	0.081	85.4
Treats as equal— Feels superior to	−0.532	122.1	0.481	61.2
Hostile towards— Dependent upon	−0.701	134.5	0.669	48.0
Submissive towards— treats as equal	0.764	40.2	−0.718	135.9
Submissive towards—admires	0.764	40.2	−0.548	123.2
Hostile towards—admires	0.258	75.0	−0.750	138.6

elements. As an illustration, we can consider the case of a male student who was assessed and briefly treated with psychotherapy for work and relationship difficulties. The clinical formulation of his problem was of an unresolved oedipal split. Success and competition with males were avoided, while relationships with women were divided between occasional brief sexual encounters, and long-term, involved, nurturant-dependent relationships. Table 13.3 lists those construct correlations which differed by an angular distance of 60° or more between the grid of self-to-other elements and the grid of other-to-self elements.

This table represents the following statement by the subject to others:

> When I am submissive to you, I am admiring and neither dependent nor inadequate; when you are submissive to me, you are not admiring, but you are dependent and inadequate. When I treat you as an equal, I am being submissive and not feeling superior; if you treat me as an equal, you are feeling superior and not submissive. My domineering behaviour is protective of you; yours is not protective of me. My submission does not imply inadequacy; yours does.

The implications, psychologically, of this pattern, would seem to be in line with the clinical formulation, for the system could be seen to be a means of maintaining a self-concept of nurturant superiority in relation to the other.

14

A Way of Looking at Psychotherapy

In earlier chapters there has been some discussion of the relationship between personal construct theory and psychoanalytic theory (Chapter 3) and some consideration of how grid data relates to psychoanalytic concepts of personality and psychotherapy. Apart from this, although much of the book has been concerned with the use of grid methods to record some of the processes and effects of psychotherapy from the point of view of both patient and therapist and to measuring change following psychotherapy, little attention has been paid to the nature of psychotherapeutic process. This process is an obscure one, and even those who have experienced it may be unable to formulate very clearly what it was that they have experienced. The analogy (the source of which I cannot recall) between psychotherapy and Columbus's journey to America often seems apt; namely, that when Columbus set out, he did not know where he was going; when he got there, he did not know where he was; and when he got back, he did not know where he had been, but he knew he had had an experience. Despite this analogy, and notwithstanding a real need for patients and therapists to endure a good deal of confusion together, I do not believe that the process is beyond rational understanding, and I believe that an account of it, in personal construct terms, may prove clarifying to some readers. It is not intended that this should be an all-embracing account so much as the provision of an additional perspective to what is already a much discussed topic, and it will focus mainly on two areas: the transference, and the problems of treating those schizoid patients who seem to make up an increasing proportion of the psychiatrist's clientèle.

In discussing psychotherapy, one must realise that many kinds of encounter, justified by divers theories, or by none at all, can lead to change. I would propose to limit the term psychotherapy to those encounters in which, unlike didactic teaching, conditioning, giving advice, or giving practical help, the aim is to alter the way in which a patient sees himself and his world. Baldly, psychotherapy can be seen to consist of the therapist's self-conscious and deliberate use of his relationship with the patient, to help the patient define and modify his construct system. Different methods of psychotherapy have, in common, the provision of a reliable, continuing relationship with either an individual therapist or a group, and most methods use language rather than other behaviours to express and explore the patient's feelings and understandings. This heavy reliance on language may be conventional rather than necessary, and the development of techniques like psychodrama, or Kelly's fixed role therapy, represent alternative approaches; but talking and listening remain the crucial components of the vast majority of psychotherapeutic encounters. In classical psychoanalysis, the virtue of this method was seen to rest on the interpretations given to the patient of childhood events, or childhood-based fantasy; the therapist's task being to provide the patient with the words and concepts with which to name and examine his situation. Through this process, the patient's confusion between his inner and outer reality was clarified, and unconscious forces (id and superego) were increasingly superseded by conscious ones. Therapists of most persuasions are aware that therapeutic change demands more than words and insights; a corrective emotional experience is also necessary. This corrective emotional experience is not something quite separate from the cognitive tasks relying upon language, for the affects which dominate the patient's experience—whether of dependency, threat, hostility, or whatever—are secondary to the patient's interpretation or construction of the nature of the relationships between himself and others. In the transference relationship of patient with therapist, the construct of the therapist as idealised patient, punitive parent, rival, or other part-object representative, will be revised not by words, but by the therapist's insistence on being himself rather than these versions offered by the patient. This revision is achieved through the emotional experience of attempting to relate to the therapist in these part-object terms, and enduring the frustration of not being allowed to. In considering how these dual therapeutic functions may be described in personal construct terms, attention may be paid to two main problems: the problem of the transference, and the concept of non-verbal constructs.

The therapist enters the patient's world as a new element, and is accommodated by the patient in his existing construct system. The construction of the therapist can be described in terms of the construct space, for example he may be seen to occupy the *clever* or *stupid*, *friendly* or *hostile* areas; and also in terms of the therapist's perceived resemblance to other elements, notably parental ones. Thus, he may be seen as being like the real, or ideal, mother or father. Initially, the therapist is usually located in an idealised area of the construct space (this is the phase of the superficial, positive transference); but sooner or later, he tends to shift to the polar negative position and, in time, may experience a varied repertoire of reciprocal roles. The therapist's first task, with the patient, is to pick up from the cues provided (cues which may include significant omissions) his current location in the patient's construct space. Having understood this, he may tell the patient what he thinks is happening, conventionally with some such phrase as, 'It seems to me you are expecting me to behave in an authoritarian way like your father used to'; and he will also consistently resist, explicitly or otherwise, the pressure put upon him by the patient to accept the roles or characteristics ascribed to him. A therapist fails his patient if he colludes with the patient by accepting the ascribed position, for, if he does this, he confirms the patient's existing structure and it is this structure which underlies the neurotic behaviour and experience.

As well as locating himself in the patient's construct system, the therapist may become aware of characteristics of the system itself; notably, a tendency to extreme polar judgments, and to idiosyncratic construct correlations such as were described in Chapter 8; and he will also be on the look-out for splitting mechanisms, knowing that if the patient locates himself or the therapist firmly at one or other extreme end of a construct dichotomy, there is likely to be distortion or denial of some aspects going on—with, perhaps, the denied qualities being attributed to an element in the polar position. The therapist will be particularly aware of ways in which qualities or affects may be segregated by the patient between the patient and himself. Here he will be encountering the primitive mechanisms of projection and introjection at work.

With many neurotic patients, there is little difficulty in understanding the patient's construct system, and in explicitly resisting collusion. Repeated interpretations, and the therapist's consistent and accepting presence, may enable the patient, in time, to achieve insight and learn less distorted, less rigid, more consensual, more complex and more effective ways of construing the self and others. For the more severely disturbed schizoid patient, however, the problem is more difficult, partly because the underlying constructs are ones acquired at a very early, pre-verbal stage of development, and partly because the schizoid defence is precisely that of avoiding all emotional experience, and this results in an attempt on the part of the patient to exclude the therapist from his world.

The nature of these powerful, pre-verbal constructs has been most elucidated by object-relations theory. Underlying the terror, helplessness, greed, envy and destructiveness of the patient trapped in the schizoid and paranoid positions, affects which are often concealed behind a false self, are implicit non-verbal constructs referring to possible constructions of self–other relationships. Commonly, these constructs refer to the basic issues of separation, trust, and power. The alternatives apparently open to the patient can be put into words something like the following: *I am abandoned by the other* versus *I am fused with, or inside the other; I am destructive of the other* versus *I will be destroyed by the other;* or *I am, or you are, full of goodness* versus *you are, or I am, full of poison.* How can the therapist get beyond the schizoid exclusion, and into a relationship whereby such constructs can be modified? Language and interpretation may, for a time, play a much less important part here than is the case with less severely ill neurotic patients. Words can be irrelevant, or even used as a potent source of confusion. For the modern, educated patient, the available schizoid texts, such as the works of Nietzsche, Kierkegaard, Kafka, and the more specifically psychiatric texts, notably those, of Laing (1960, 1961), provide an eloquent, ready-made vocabulary of despair which can itself operate as part of a false system, being used to mask and distract from the patient's real, direct experience of his problem. Therapists also may use words as a defence. In my view, the therapist who maintains a strictly orthodox, detached stance, keeping his personal self inscrutable, can provide a chilling mirror to the defended schizoid patient. These patients must grapple with the reality of another before they can accept the reality of their own feelings, a reality not to be confused with the therapist being 'all good' or departing from the ultimately necessary and reassuring conventions of the treatment situation and relationship. The 'holding function of the therapist'—to use Winnicott's phrase—is to provide a degree of reliable human presence within the safety of which the defensive retreat from involvement and feeling can be gradually discarded. Once this has been achieved, and an emotional contact with the therapist has been achieved, then both patient and therapist must be prepared for a stormy relationship, and the task of the therapist is to be exposed to this and to demonstrate in action that he can survive the patient's attacks, that his fund of goodness is enough to balance the badness, and that he can allow separation without this being experienced by the patient as simple abandonment. That this process is not achieved through words alone is clear from the accounts for example of Milner (1969) and of Blake (1968). Constructs of mutual destructiveness can be revised only through the *experience* of mutual survival, and constructs of fusion or abandonment can be modified only by the *experience* of separation without loss of relationship and by the establishment of clear boundaries between the self and other. This experience is real to both patient and therapist—the situation providing for each, in different ways, safeties which can allow the patient's primitive feelings to be experienced and worked with. As therapy proceeds, the importance of words to describe, comprehend and redefine the relationship increases, but the revision of constructs is achieved through the experience first, and by words after.

Such understanding of the psychotherapeutic process as is available has been derived from the experience of therapists who have sat for long hours over long months or years with patients, and who have puzzled over the relationships which have developed. The theories which psychoanalysis has offered to justify and explain this process have developed and changed, and have become inextricably linked with theories of personality development. This link has been a highly creative one, and indeed, the attempted reconstruction of infantile experience offered by analytic theory seems to provide the only comprehensible explanation for the origin of some of the pre-verbal constructs described above; but the mixng of developmental psychology with an account of a therapeutic process has served at times to confuse the general understanding of what goes on during therapy, and because the developmental theory itself has often been seen to be complex, obscure and in many ways, untestable, rejection of this aspect has often led to incomprehension of the claims of psychoanalysis to assist in the process of cure. Even analysts themselves are strangely ambivalent in the claims they make in this field.

It is possible to look at the therapeutic process quite independently of any developmental theory, even though it may often be a comfort for the therapist to be able to link his present experience of the patient with a formulation about the patient's past. Much psychotherapeutic change is achieved through relationships based on theories which most would regard as palpably false—such as in the work of witch-doctors; or through processes which show an exclusive concern with the present interaction, such as Rogerian counselling, or much group therapy. It seems, therefore, that the fundamental nature of the help offered by a therapist is through his entry into the patient's world in the present, as an agent and explorer and an accepting survivor, rather than as an oppressor, victim, or pawn. The therapist's movement through the patient's world may occur within a variety of settings, and the relationship may be circumscribed by a variety of rituals, the significance of which we do not know; but whatever these may be, once the therapist is in the patient's world, his role and responsibility are clear: he must provide conditions in which the patient can get on with the task of loosening and rebuilding his construct system. In psychoanalytic terms, these conditions are designed to allow, in the words of Rycroft (1968) 'a special form of relationship . . . in which the analyst, while remaining an external object, can also become the temporary representation and personification of the various internal figures dating from the past . . .' In the course of this change process, the patient may rediscover some good and some resource in himself, and in his past, which he had lost sight of, but— particularly in the case of the very sick patient—the therapist and others in the patient's world, if there be any, must also be prepared to provide some good in the present, too. The persistence called for in the treatment of a severely ill schizoid patient gives evidence of the immense power and self-perpetuating inertia of those constructs established at the start of life. It is my belief that psychoanalysis is right in stressing that the comprehension of powerful infantile constructs is crucial to understanding human experience and behaviour; it is my hope that the techniques described in this book may have some part to play in clarifying the ways in which these constructs can dominate present experience and behaviour, and how they may be identified and changed.

15

Future Developments

In the preceding chapters, I have given a partial view of the
current status of personal construct theory and repertory grid research; partial, both in the sense of being incomplete, and in the
sense of being selective in its concentration upon those areas of the
field which have particularly appealed to me, namely, the
clinical applications of the technique and the connections with
psychotherapy and psychoanalysis. In this last chapter, it is my
intention to give a correspondingly partial evaluation of the
possible future potential of grid technique and personal construct
theory, written in the consciousness that a great deal of varied
work by many other people is in progress, and that my own involvement is also leading in diverse directions.

Application of Existing RG Techniques

It seems likely that the forms of repertory grid technique already developed will find their way increasingly into the reper-
toires of clinical psychologists. Mounting pressure on psychiatric
and social work resources, and an increasing willingness among
clinicians and experimentalists to replace polemic and dogmatism
with attempts at evaluation and rational comparison, are likely to
encourage more research into the indications for and effects of
clinical intervention. In this work outcome studies, using 'before
and after' grid measures, and process studies using grid records
of on-going therapeutic interactions—whether individual, conjoint, or group—and recording serially the perceptions of both
patients and therapists, seem likely to play an important part.
The combination of these grid-based methods with parallel
evaluations of change, using measures of symptoms and social
incapacity, and with other modes of assessing the processes of
change, such as the analysis of tape or video-tape excerpts of
treatment sessions, could bring greater depth to the vexed field
of psychotherapy research.

In the search for better understanding of the psychoses, grid methods, so far, have been largely restricted to the use of the standard Bannister–Fransella grid test of thought disorder (Bannister, 1960, 1962; Bannister & Fransella 1966), although some of the assumptions behind this test have been questioned (McFadyen & Foulds 1972; Frith & Lillie 1972). In the future, it would be of value to employ more flexible grid methods to investigate psychotic thought processes. The use of people known to the patient, rather than photographs, as elements has been shown to be more sensitive to the schizophrenic's difficulty in psychological construing (Williams & Quirke 1972). The consideration of both construct and element relationships, as in the study of the hypomanic patient by Rowe (1971c), mentioned in Chapter 9, is also likely to provide material of greater interest than is the use of standard techniques. The nature of the schizophrenic's conceptual difficulties, and the characteristic modes of construing found in other psychoses and in those with marked neurotic disorders, is likely to be further explored by the methods of displaying construct structure developed by Makhlouf-Norris *et al.* (1970, 1973) which were discussed briefly in Chapter 13. The structure of the construct system as analysed by this method (between monolithic, articulated, segmented) of different diagnostic groups and the relation of this aspect of the construct system to the patient's response to different treatments may prove a fruitful research area. Bender (unpublished paper), using this approach, has demonstrated some of the characteristic patterns of different diagnostic groups in a large psychotic population.

Application of existing forms of grid technique outside the strictly clinical field is also likely to increase. Children appear to be able to employ grid techniques satisfactorily (see Leach 1971; Howarth 1972) and a systematic study of change and development in children's construct systems would seem to be of great potential interest, representing a way of extending work in the tradition of Piaget and, in particular, of paying more attention to individual differences.

In sociology and anthropology—where perceptions of role and caste are often of central concern—the capacity of grid technique to elicit the subject's own judgments in his own terms would seem to be of value.

Variations in Grid Techniques

It is unlikely that the existing repertory grid techniques will be the only ones used in the future, for one of the great advantages of grid methodology is its flexibility. People drawn to the personal construct approach are unlikely to yield to the temptation to reduce the technique to the level of a set of standardised tests, and are likely to be attracted by its capacity to generate more data than is expected, rather than less. Certain aspects of the technique do, however, deserve further research. Simple reliability studies are still sparse, and little is known about the effects of the setting, the tester's instructions and manner, or the mode of elicitation of constructs and elements, upon the range of elements and constructs produced by subjects. The degree to which the particular element pool selected may modify, or determine, the choice and range of constructs and construct interrelationships is also an unresearched area. The form of test used, between dichotomising, ranking and rating of elements, may also, as Mair & Boyd (1967) have shown, influence the results. Forms of analysis of basic grid data and ways of displaying revealed relationships may continue to multiply, though the programs developed by Slater have already reached a high degree of sophistication without demanding complexity from either subject or experimenter, and seem likely to remain the main resource in this field.

Development of Theory

How far personal construct theory will be developed and elaborated remains uncertain; it is a strange fact that, despite the large claims made for the uniqueness and superordinacy of personal construct theory by its most enthusiastic adherents, its basic postulates and ten corollaries receive little critical attention, and tend to reappear almost as an incantation, in unchanged form from publication to publication. This lack of interest in the refinement and validation of the theory may represent a healthy scepticism towards the larger claims made for it, or may just reflect the fact that in psychology, as in other sciences, fascination with new available techniques often proves a more potent stimulus to research than does a new theoretical formulation. That the technology available through the grid can be, and is at times, specifically deployed to test aspects of the theory is true; but, as I have tried to show, the technique can equally well be deployed and interpreted in relation to practices and theories owing nothing to Kelly. The real power of the grid technique is that it gives the subject a chance to disclose a lot about himself in a short time. What he discloses may be made sense of by any theory claiming to be a human psychology. In the human sciences, the spectacle of a lot of relatively hard data in search of a theory to explain it, rather than a lot of theory waiting somewhat helplessly or hopelessly, for some data to test it, is perhaps a refreshing sight, though theoreticians would doubtless regard this as an heretical viewpoint.

Using RG Techniques to Explore and Educate

The use of grid techniques in education seems potentially of considerable interest. Teaching and learning are concerned, essentially, with the elaboration of concepts (constructs), and only secondarily with the accumulation of facts (elements). Didactic teaching consists of feeding the pupil with facts and concepts, ready-made. Such an approach may fail, in its own terms, through neglecting to explore first the nature and capacity of the pupil's pre-existing construct system; and it is bound to fail by any criteria which measure the pupil's capacity to cope with new information. The creative act, whether in art or science, is one in which new frameworks and patterns are applied to phenomena, and didactic teaching denies the student the experience of converting his bewilderment at inadequately comprehended data into the search for new ways of construction. This observation links with the debate about convergent–divergent thinking, to which Hudson (1966) has directed attention, and with Snyder's (1971) analysis of the anxieties and disillusions of students whose creativity can so easily be drowned in data. Grid techniques can play a part, diagnostically, in the teaching situation, in that the initial constructs of students in relation to a given field can be explored by them. This diagnostic process—of value to the teacher, whatever teaching method is to be used—becomes in itself a learning technique also, as soon as feedback of the students' different individual constructions is given to a group, for this can provide them with a living experience of the need to scan alternative constructions. I have employed this approach in a small way at the start of a seminar course with psychology postgraduate students, to investigate how different psychological theories were construed by the students. At a more elaborate level, it would seem theoretically possible to design a learning programme designed, not primarily to test and reinforce correct solutions, but rather to confront the student with the need to scan, select and elaborate new ways of construing the data. As with more conventional programmed learning, one of the main benefits of such an approach might prove to be the thinking demanded of the teacher in the construction of the programme.

Apart from the possible use of grid techniques in formal education, they can be of value in confronting people with insights about themselves. At the simplest level, the feedback of grid data to a subject who has carried out some form of grid test, may be of value to him in the search for self-understanding, and the grid's conversion of judgments into numerical measures or geographical representations may provide a useful new set of metaphors with which to consider human dilemmas. Thus, if I do not know how to choose in a situation, or if I feel oppressed or troubled by the choice I have to make, it may help me to state the polar constructs which are defining and underlying my position; through my examination of them, I may discover that I am trapped in a false dichotomy, or seeking to resolve an issue within an inappropriately selected or transferred segment of my construct system. If another fails to behave as I predict, it may be that I am guilty of crude misidentification, in the sense of locating them incorrectly with reference to another figure in my construct space; or it may be that I am fortunate in that I am encountering that valuable and rare other who can surprise me in a way that demands that I extend and make more complicated the system through which I operate. If I find myself discarding evidence which fails to confirm my predictions, and if I can learn to monitor this process before it is complete, then I must suspect that my need to maintain a stable system is more powerful than my need to develop an effective one. Any individual or group committed to puzzling constructively over interpersonal processes may, I believe, gain something from the use of grid technique as a basis for discussion or introspection. For example, a marital couple, faced with their alternative constructions of their own relationship, may be able to use this revealed difference to clarify their difficulties; or a therapist, attempting to predict a patient's grid, or examining the way in which he construes his patients (see Chapter 12) may be faced with his counter-transference with a degree of clarity which he may find helpful, if uncomfortable. A team of nurses looking after a group of psychiatric patients may find, through doing a grid together, how differently they view and respond to their charges, and may be able to use this sharing to achieve a rounder vision of their involvement with patients. In these, and doubtless in many other ways, the grid offers a way of gaining insight and exploring possibilities. As I have emphasised, especially in Chapter 14, such insights alone do not necessarily lead to change, especially where the ego is highly defended; but there are times at which, and circumstances within which, insight, especially if shared, can be utilised. Grid data, in presenting a view of the self to the self, can reveal the ways in which some impossibilities are idiosyncratic and personally determined, and hence can open the way to new possibilities. The portrait of the self offered by the Kellian mirror seems to provoke something of the optimism which Kelly gave expression to in his philosophical stance of 'constructive alternativism'. I hope readers who have got this far will share something of the optimism I feel about the potential value to human psychology of the methods derived from Kelly, which have been described in this book.

References

Adams-Webber, J. R. (1969). 'Cognitive Complexity and Sociality'. *Brit. J. Soc. Clin. Psychol.*, 8, 211.

Adams-Webber, J. R. (1970). 'Elicited Versus Provided Constructs in Repertory Grid Technique—a Review'. *Brit. J. Med. Psychol.*, 43, 349.

Bannister, D. (1960). 'Conceptual Structures in Thought-Disordered Schizophrenics'. *J. Ment. Sci.*, 106, 1230.

Bannister, D. (1962). 'The Nature and Measurement of Schizophrenic Thought Disorder'. *J. Ment. Sci.*, 108, 825.

Bannister, D. & Fransella, F. (1966). 'A Grid Test of Schizophrenic Thought Disorder'. *Brit. J. Clin. Psychol.*, 5, 95.

Bannister, D. & Fransella, F. (1971). *Inquiring Man: The Theory of Personal Constructs* (London: Penguin Books)

Bannister, D. & Mair, J. M. M. (1968). *The Evaluation of Personal Constructs* (London: Academic Press)

Berger, P. L. & Luckman, T. (1967). *The Social Construction of Reality* (London: Allen Lane. The Penguin Press)

Blake, Y. (1968). 'Psychotherapy and the More Disturbed Patient'. *Brit. J. Med. Psychol.*, 41, 199.

Bonarius, J. C. J. (1965). 'Research in the Personal Construct Theory of George A. Kelly: Role Construct Repertory Test and Basic Theory'. In B. Maher (ed.) *Progress in Experimental Psychology*, 2nd Ed., Vol. 2. (London: Academic Press)

Bonarius, J. C. J. (1970). 'Fixed Role Therapy: a Double Paradox'. *Brit. J. Med. Psychol.*, 43, 213.

Chomsky, N. (1968). *Language and Mind* (New York: Harcourt, Brace and World Inc.)

Clowes, M. (1972). 'Man the Creative Machine: a Perspective from Artificial Intelligence'. (Address to the I.C.A. February 1972)

Crisp, A. H. (1964). 'An Attempt to Measure an Aspect of "Transference" '. *Brit. J. Med. Psychol.*, 37, 17.

Crown, S. & Crisp, A. H. (1966). 'A Short Clinical Diagnostic Self-Rating Scale for Psychoneurotic Patients'. *Brit. J. Psychiat.*, 112, 917.

Dicks, H. V. (1967). *Marital Tension* (London: Routledge & Kegan Paul)

Fairbairn, W. R. D. (1952). *Psychoanalytic Studies of the Personality* (London: Tavistock)

Fransella, F. & Adams, B. (1965). 'An Illustration of the Use of Repertory Grid Technique in a Clinical Setting'. *Brit. J. Soc. Clin. Psychol.*, 5, 51.

Frith, C. D. & Lillie, F. J. (1972). 'Why Does the Repertory Grid Test Indicate Thought Disorder'. *Brit. J. Soc. Clin. Psychol.*, 11, 33.

Gombrich, E. H. (1960). *Art and Illusion* (London: Phaidon Press)

Guntrip, H. (1971). *Psychoanalytic Theory, Therapy and the Self* (London: Hogarth Press)

Hinkle, D. N. (1968). In *The Evaluation of Personal Constructs*, ed. Bannister, D. (London: Academic Press)

Holland, R. (1970). 'George Kelly: Constructive Innocent and Reluctant Existentialist'. In *Perspectives in Personal Construct Theory*, ed. Bannister, D. (London: Academic Press)

Howarth, R. V. (1972). 'The Psychiatry of Terminal Illness in Children'. *Proc. Roy. Soc. Med.*, 65, 1039.

Hudson, L. (1966). *Contrary Imaginations* (London: Methuen)

Jahoda, M. (1972). 'Social Psychology and Psychoanalysis: A Mutual Challenge'. *Bull. Brit. Psychol. Soc.*, 25, 269.

James, W. (1911). *Some Problems of Philosophy* (London: Longmans Green & Co.)

Kagan, J. (1958). 'The Concept of Identification'. *Psychol. Rev.*, 65, 296.

Klein, M. (1948). *Contributions to Psychoanalysis* (London: Hogarth Press)

Klein, M. (1957). *Envy and Gratitude* (London: Tavistock Press)

Kelly, G. A. (1955). *The Psychology of Personal Constructs* (New York: Norton)

Kelly, G. A. (1963). *A Theory of Personality* (New York: Norton)

Kreitman, N. (1962). 'Mental Disorder in Married Couples'. *J. Ment. Sci.*, 108, 438.

Kreitman, N. (1968). 'Married Couples Admitted to Mental Hospitals'. *Brit. J. Psychiat.*, 114, 699.

Kreitman, N., Collins, J., Nelson, B. & Troop, J. (1970). 'Neurosis and Marital Interaction'. *Brit. J. Psychiat.*, 117, 33.

Lacan, J. (1966). *Écrits* 1 (Paris: Editions du Seuil)

Laing, R. D. (1960). *The Divided Self* (London: Tavistock)

Laing, R. D. (1961). *The Self and Others* (London: Tavistock)

Leach, D. (1971). 'Understanding Reading Retardation'. Dissertation for the Master's Degree in Educational Psychology, University of Sussex.

Leman, G. (1970). 'Words and Worlds'. In *Perspectives in Personal Construct Theory*, ed. Bannister, D. (London: Academic Press)

Lévi-Strauss, C. (1966). *The Savage Mind* (London: Weidenfeld & Nicolson)

McFadyen, M. & Foulds, G. A. (1972). 'Comparison of Provided and Elicited Grid Content in the Grid Test of Schizophrenic Thought Disorder'. *Brit. J. Psychiat.*, 121, 53.

McPherson, F. M. & Walton, H. J. (1970). 'The Dimensions of Psychotherapy Group Interaction: an Analysis of Clinicians' Constructs'. *Brit. J. Med. Psychol.*, 43, 281.

Main, T. F. (1966). 'Mutual Projection in a Marriage'. *Comprehensive Psychiatry*, 7, 432.

Mair, J. M. M. & Boyd, P. R. (1967). 'A Comparison of Two Grid Forms'. *Brit. J. Soc. Clin. Psychol.*, 6, 220.

Makhlouf-Norris, F., Gwynne Hones, H. & Norris, H. (1970). 'Articulation of the Conceptual Structure in Obsessional Neurosis'. *Brit. J. Soc. Clin. Psychol.* 9, 264.

Makhlouf-Norris, F. & Norris, H. (1973). 'The Obsessive-Compulsive Syndrome as a Neurotic Device for the Reduction of Self-Uncertainty'. *Brit. J. Psychiat.*, 122, 277.

Malan, D. H. (1963). *A Study of Brief Psychotherapy* (London: Tavistock)

Milner, M. (1969). *The Hands of the Living God: An Account of a Psycho-analytic Treatment* (London: Hogarth)

Mowrer, O. H. (1950). *Learning Theory and Personality Dynamics* (New York: Ronald Press)

Pond, D. A., Ryle, A. & Hamilton, M. (1963). 'Marriage and Neurosis in a Working Class Population'. *Brit. J. Psychiat.*, 109, 592.

Rowe, D. (1969). 'Estimates of Change in a Depressive Patient'. *Brit. J. Psychiat.*, 115, 527, 1199–1200.

Rowe, D. (1971a). 'An Examination of a Psychiatrist's Predictions of a Patient's Constructs'. *Brit. J. Psychiat.*, 118, 543, 231–44.

Rowe, D. (1971b). 'Poor Prognosis in a Case of Depression as Predicted by the Repertory Grid'. *Brit. J. Psychiat.*, 118, 544, 297–300.

Rowe, D. (1971c). 'Changes in the Perception of Relationships in the Hypomanic State as Shown by the Repertory Grid'. *Brit. J. Psychiat.*, 119, 550, 323–4.

Rycroft, C. (1968). 'An Enquiry into the Function of Words in the Psychoanalytic Situation'. In *Imagination and Reality* (London: Hogarth Press)

Ryle, A. (1967). 'A Repertory Grid Study of the Meaning and Consequences of a Suicidal Act'. *Brit. J. Psychiat.*, 113, 1393–1403.

Ryle, A. (1969). 'The Psychology and Psychiatry of Academic Difficulty in Students'. *Proc. Roy. Soc. Med.*, 62, 1263.

Ryle, A. & Breen, D. (1971). 'The Recognition of Psychopathology on the Repertory Grid'. *Brit. J. Psychiat.*, 119, 319.

Ryle, A. & Breen, D. (1972a). 'Some Differences in the Personal Constructs of Neurotic and Normal Subjects'. *Brit. J. Psychiat.*, 120, 483.

Ryle, A. & Breen, D. (1972b). 'A Comparison of Adjusted and Maladjusted Couples Using the Double Dyad Grid'. *Brit. J. Med. Psychol.*, 45, 375.

Ryle, A. & Breen, D. (1972c). 'The Use of the Double Dyad Grid in the Clinical Setting'. *Brit. J. Med. Psychol.*, 45, 383.

Ryle, A. & Breen, D. (1974). 'Change in the Course of Social-Work Training: A Repertory Grid Study'. *Brit. J. Med. Psychol.*, 47,139.

Ryle, A. & Lunghi, M. (1969). 'The Measurement of Relevant Change After Psychotherapy—Use of Repertory Grid Testing'. *Brit. J. Psychiat.*, 115, 1297.

Ryle, A. & Lunghi, M. (1970). 'The Dyad Grid: A Modification of Repertory Grid Technique'. *Brit. J. Psychiat.*, 117, 323.

Ryle, A. & Lunghi, M. (1971). 'A Therapist's Prediction of a Patient's Dyad Grid'. *Brit. J. Psychiat.*, 118, 555.

Ryle, A. & Lunghi, M. (1972). 'Parental and Sex Role Identification of Students Measured with a Repertory Grid Technique'. *Brit. J. Soc. Clin. Psychol.*, 11, 149.

Shotter, J. (1970). 'Men, the Man Makers. George Kelly and the Psychology of Personal Constructs'. In *Perspectives in Personal Construct Theory*, ed. Bannister, D. (London: Academic Press)

Slater, P. (1969). 'Theory and Technique of the Repertory Grid'. *Brit. J. Psychiat.*, 115, 1287–96.

Slater, P. (1972). 'The Measurement of Consistency in Repertory Grids'. *Brit. J. Psychiat.*, 121, 45.

Smail, D. J. (1972). 'A Grid Measure of Empathy in a Therapeutic Group'. *Brit. J. Med. Psychol.*, 45, 165.

Snyder, N. (1971). *The Hidden Curriculum* (New York: Knopf)

Tharp, R. G. (1963). 'Psychological Patterns in Marriage'. *Psychol. Bulletin*, 60, 2.

Truax, C. B., Wargo, D. G., Frank, J. D., Imber, S. D., Battle, C. C., Hoehn-Saric, R., Nash, E. & Stone, A. (1966). 'Therapist Empathy, Genuineness and Warmth and Patient Therapeutic Outcome'. *J. Consult. Psychol.*, 30, 395.

Watson, J. P. (1970). 'A Measure of Therapist–Patient Understanding'. *Brit. J. Psychiat.*, 117, 319.

Watson, J. P. (1972). 'Possible Measures of Change During Group Psychotherapy'. *Brit. J. Med. Psychol.*, 45, 71.

Williams, E. & Quirke, C. (1972). 'Psychological Construing in Schizophrenics'. *Brit. J. Med. Psychol.*, 45, 79.

Winch, R. F. (1958). *Mate Selection* (New York: Harper)

Index